THE BIBLE IN 52 WEEKS WORKBOOK

A YEARLONG BIBLE STUDY FOR WOMEN

the BIBLE IN 52 WEEKS WORKBOOK

A YEARLONG BIBLE STUDY FOR WOMEN

REV. BRITTINI L. PALMER

Series Designer: Liz Cosgrove
Art Director: Lisa Schreiber
Art Producers: Sue Bischofberger and Stacey Stambaugh
Editor: Adrian Potts
Production Designer: Martin Worthington
Production Editors: Caroline Flanagan and Rachel Taenzler
Production Manager: Riley Hoffman

All biblical verses are used as reflected in the Common English Bible version of the Christian Bible unless otherwise noted.

Published by Callisto Publishing LLC C/O Sourcebooks LLC
P.O. Box 4410, Naperville, Illinois 60567-4410
(630) 961-3900
callistopublishing.com

Printed in the United States of America

This book is dedicated to
my grandmother, Dolly Ilantha Palmer (1936–2011),
and Nana, Willie Mae Lamons (1938–2020).
They were divine, audacious, beautiful women
who cared for me.

CONTENTS

INTRODUCTION

I INVITE YOU INTO THIS 52-WEEK BIBLE STUDY EXPERIENCE. Like many challenges we face, reading the entire Bible is no easy task—trust me, I know from experience. This workbook makes it easier by giving you a year-long road map to deepen your understanding of scripture and your connection to God with the help of reflections, prompts, prayers, and activities. As you begin your journey, I extend an open invitation to be exactly who you are at this moment. So relax and embrace the incredible ways of engaging with God.

I am extremely honored to walk with you. As a writer, ordained minister, and communications consultant, I write, preach, and communicate remembering the lessons I've learned as a Black woman in the world. In 2011, when I first accepted my call to ministry, my pastor—Reverend Tyrone Nelson of the historic Sixth Mount Zion Baptist Church, in Richmond, Virginia—asked me if I had ever read the entire Bible. The answer was no. After this conversation, I unplugged my TV and read the Bible every day after I got off work. While studying for licensure, I was able to preach, lead Bible study classes, and assist with various ministries. I also joined a women's Bible study class led by Reverend Dwylene Butler. In a life-giving way, I was able to connect my reality to stories in the Bible. In this space we were able to affirm, challenge, and support each other. The way I engaged with my family, colleagues, strangers, and myself helped me grow in God's love and light.

With spiritual guidance and family support, I moved to Atlanta, Georgia, in 2016 to attend seminary. During this time in my life, I consistently prayed for wisdom. I served as a community and social justice intern and associate minister at Lakewood Church of Hope (where I was ordained); provided spiritual services to women and children experiencing homelessness and poverty at a Christian nonprofit for four years; and became the communication coordinator for the RISE Together Mentorship Network, an organization founded by Rev. Dr. Lisa D. Rhodes that connects, supports, and empowers women of color ministry leaders across the globe.

Through the instruction of brilliant religious scholars, personal experience, and prayer, God has given me the words to share and inspire others, and this is my prayer for all of you. There may be times when you don't feel like reading, and that's okay. I am encouraging you to read anyway and be kind to yourself. We all are walking "Bibles"; our lives are wrapped up in the sacred text. My hope is that as you return to the Bible each week in the year ahead, you can stretch, learn, and grow as you find yourself in the Word of God.

HOW TO USE THIS BOOK

This workbook is designed to encourage all readers to engage and learn from the entire Bible in one year. You will be tackling scripture in very manageable portions, helping you get used to reading and spending time in the Word daily.

WHAT IS THE BIBLE?

I remember telling a friend, "The Bible is like a reality TV show." You never really know what you will get when you open it up. It may be entertaining, sad, or funny; you may agree or disagree with what you read.

The Bible has taken many "shapes" over the centuries and has been used to give hope, love, and ways to navigate the world. The Bible has also been used in inaccurate, misleading ways to cause division and justify pain. In this same book, you can find stories full of questions, scandals, and inspiration. You will find historical and prophetic writings, prose, poetry, and so much more. It is important to remember the Bible was written during specific time periods, driven primarily by male perspectives, and intended for specific audiences.

The Bible has been translated into countless languages globally. In this workbook, most of the scriptural references come from the Common English Bible (CEB) translation, unless otherwise noted. Always feel free to use whatever translation you are most comfortable with. The Bible was often read in mass, and this book continues in that tradition. The power is not in the physical book itself, but the unveiling of the stories—often stories of women. The power comes from spending time with the stories, investigating areas of tension, and locating yourself in the pages you read. Regardless of your denomination or social location, there is something for you in this book.

WHAT'S IN THIS WORKBOOK?

This book is designed as a companion to *The Bible in 52 Weeks: A Yearlong Bible Study for Women*. This workbook goes deeper into the weekly readings, themes, and lessons of that book and provides additional questions and activities.

The Bible is no short book. To make this journey more manageable, the Bible readings will only be a few pages and should take about 15 to 20 minutes each.

You will see the readings are not in strict chronological order. You don't have to wait for months to get to the splendor of the gospels or the grandeur of the psalms—they'll pop up at different points throughout the year. You may also enjoy the visions of the Old Testament prophet one week and some of Paul's letters to the church the next.

WHAT MATERIALS DO I NEED?

This book.

The Bible. Use any version or translation you'd like. You may also benefit from an electronic or audio version that can be downloaded on your phone.

Notebook, journal, or iPad. This will be helpful if you want to take extra notes.

Pen or pencil.

LEARN AND GROW

As women, we know many things can deter us from taking care of ourselves. Reading the Bible can be a practice of spiritual self-care. As you take this journey, remember to take your time and be gentle with yourself. Engage with the Bible in ways that feel true to who you are. As you read daily, pray for guidance and revelation. Every day is a new day to learn more about God's activity in the world and in your life.

WEEK 1

THERE'S NOTHING TOO HARD FOR GOD!

READINGS

Reading 1: Genesis 1–4

Reading 2: Genesis 5–8

Reading 3: Genesis 9–12

Reading 4: Genesis 13–15

Reading 5: Genesis 16–18

Reading 6: Genesis 19–21

FROM THE VERY BEGINNING GOD WAS PRESENT and active. The beautiful yet complex book of Genesis offers insight into the origins of the world, the imagination of God, and where we fit in. The narratives are written with the troubles and triumphs of the audience in mind. We read of creation, human activity, sin, genealogies, flood stories, covenants, tests and trials, curses and blessings, beginnings, and death. From the exploitation of the environment to the mistreatment of women, we hear of the complexities present in the world.

The stories in Genesis allow us to see that, no matter what has happened to us, we can always begin again and lean into our lives to grow. God's universal action lands right in our living rooms.

When we feel like giving up due to the pressures of the world, we must remember to look around and listen. Let us not treat each other as Sarai treated Hagar and the world treated them both. Let us remember the words of biblical scholar Dr. Renita Weems, who calls on us to explore possibilities for divine healing, because there is nothing too hard for God!

REFLECTION QUESTIONS

1. **Genesis 1–4:** How does knowing that God created everything good make you look at the world differently?

2. **Genesis 5–8:** What did you learn about God's protection from reading the story of Noah?

3. **Genesis 9–12:** How do you see God's covenant with people and every living thing today?

4. **Genesis 13–15:** What are some of Abraham's characteristics you see in Genesis 14?

5. **Genesis 16–18:** Like Abraham and Sarah, in what ways can you be more available to receive what God has for you?

6. **Genesis 19–21:** God hears our cries, just as he heard Hagar's. When has God answered your cries? Have you taken time to enjoy creation? What are you thankful for?

POINTS TO PONDER

1. Since we are all a part of God's creation, God declares we are good and worthy. How do you honor this by taking care of yourself?
2. Have you ever been mistreated by another woman? What did God reveal to you to help you move forward?
3. Have you created anything lately that brings you joy?

ACTIVITY

Write a short prayer to help guide you through any problems.

1. Grab a piece of paper and a pen. List everything in your life that feels challenging.
2. Using your list, write a prayer to reflect on during this season. Start with, "Dear God, help me face these challenges and lean on you. Some of these challenges are..."
3. Conclude the prayer with, "I trust you, God, and I know that nothing is too hard for you. Amen."

GUIDED PRAYER

God, allow me to experience your creation. Allow those I journey with and me to rest, declaring we are more than conquerors and are good. In the name of Jesus, Amen.

WEEK 2

GIVING UP IS NOT AN OPTION

READINGS

Reading 1: Genesis 22–25

Reading 2: Genesis 26–29

Reading 3: Genesis 30–33

Reading 4: Genesis 34–36

Reading 5: Genesis 37–41

Reading 6: Genesis 42–46

IN THIS WEEK'S READINGS, we see women like Sarah and Rachel faced with unfair expectations, trying to make things work. Sometimes, when this happens to us, we are prone to making bad decisions, placing the people we love in danger, sacrificing our purpose, or giving up when we should keep going. Giving up is not just stopping but sometimes intentionally going in the wrong direction. We have a task in front of us that seems hard, so we ignore it and try something else. We start a passion project, but when fear creeps in we do something easier. Have you ever experienced this?

With the pressures and uncertainties of this world, it's easy to give up, and yet giving up is being disloyal to God. This is hard when situations don't feel or sound like blessings; we can ask Esau about this. Esau put his physical desires in front of his blessing and birthright. He gave up what God wanted him to have. He was later tricked by his own mother and brother. But what we learn is that God has a way of making what should cause heartache into a space of healing and restoration. It is when we don't give up that we open up pathways for God to do God's work. In Genesis 24, Rebekah said, "I will go." She made a choice. Make a choice today to not give up, remembering your gifts always make room for you. Yes, we often face evil realities, but whatever you do, just don't give up.

REFLECTION QUESTIONS

1. **Genesis 22–25:** Sarah lived until she was 127 years old. Why don't you think she gave up?

2. **Genesis 26–29:** Rebekah was very involved in the blessings of Jacob and Isaac. How was she trying to serve God?

3. **Genesis 30–33:** Like Rachel, we all experience jealousy and hopelessness. How can you relate?

4. **Genesis 34–36:** How did God speak through the devastation in these chapters?

5. **Genesis 37–41:** In Genesis 39, Joseph was tempted yet able to think clearly in the moment. What can you learn from this?

6. **Genesis 42–46:** What does the story of Joseph reuniting with his brothers teach you about not giving up?

POINTS TO PONDER

1. What jumped out at you from this week's readings and why?
2. We sometimes go after things we think will fulfill us and never realize other paths and directions we could take. How might this be true for you?
3. Has anyone tried to kill your dreams? Did you do this to someone else? What did you learn?

ACTION OF THE WEEK

Consider a practical challenge you've always wanted to try. It could be anything from exercising five days in a row, going rock climbing, cooking an exotic dish—the possibilities are endless! Choose something that pushes you. Commit to completing the task this week and hold yourself accountable. Let this experience reflect how you want to approach life moving forward.

GUIDED PRAYER

Dear God, thank you for working behind the scenes on my behalf. Thank you for your provision. Help me daily to hear you and never give up. Amen.

WEEK 3

EVERYTHING IS PURPOSEFUL

READINGS

Reading 1: Genesis 47–50

Reading 2: Exodus 1–3

Reading 3: Exodus 4–7

Reading 4: Exodus 8–11

Reading 5: Exodus 12–15

Reading 6: Exodus 16–18

IN THIS WEEK'S READINGS, Joseph and his family come back together. As Joseph fulfills his duty to the crown, his family multiplies while experiencing the blessing and death of their beloved Jacob. The events that lead to their deliverance and establishment reveal that the journey is not easy, and yet God can give us what we need—even when we can't see it.

As I reflect, there have been many times when I've been stressed due to the conditions around me, which made it hard to see what God was doing in my life. In Exodus 1, the two midwives Shiphrah and Puah stood united and chose to save Moses. They refused to let corrupt orders interfere with their purpose. Perhaps they, too, knew what it was like to feel stressed and trapped in their routines, and yet they had no idea their actions would lead to their descendants' walk toward freedom.

Staying steadfast in the face of distractions helps what may seem pointless become purposeful.

The journey is the hard part. Walk with pride and purpose to newfound freedom, remembering what God said to Moses in Exodus 3:14: "I am who I am."

REFLECTION QUESTIONS

1. **Genesis 47–50:** Before Jacob's passing, he blessed his family. How does this imply everything is purposeful?

2. **Exodus 1–3:** God has a way of getting our attention, just as God did for Moses with the burning bush. What is God trying to tell you?

3. **Exodus 4–7:** Like Moses and the shepherd's rod, sometimes what we need is right in front of us. What could you be overlooking in life?

4. **Exodus 8–11:** The hardening of Pharaoh's heart occurs many times in Exodus. When has your heart hardened? Why?

5. **Exodus 12–15:** The song of Miriam is regarded as one of the oldest Israelite poems in existence. What older songs keep you going?

6. **Exodus 16–18:** What is the significance of Aaron holding Moses's hands up in order to defeat the warriors of Amalek?

POINTS TO PONDER

1. Like Moses, we all have a testimony. What is your testimony?
2. Do you sometimes feel like your children, age, or experiences have pushed you away from your purpose?
3. What song helps or encourages you and why?

VERSE OF THE WEEK

Reflect on Exodus 14:13: "Moses answered the people, 'Do not be afraid. Stand firm and you will see the deliverance the Lord will bring you today.'" Draw encouragement from these words to stand firm and trust in God.

GUIDED PRAYER

Dear God, when others try to diminish my dreams, help me see the bigger picture. Help me lean on you as I walk toward freedom. Amen.

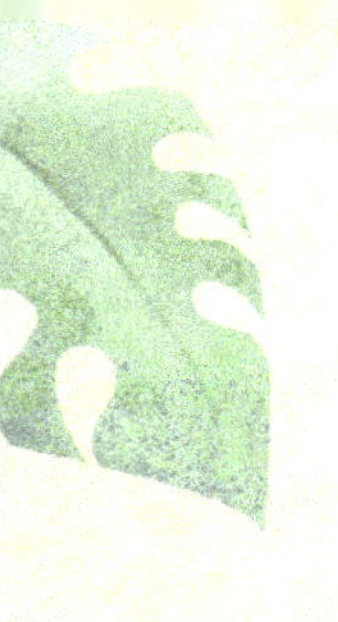

WEEK 4

THANK GOD FOR THE CRUSHING

READINGS

Reading 1: Exodus 19–21

Reading 2: Exodus 22–25

Reading 3: Exodus 26–29

Reading 4: Exodus 30–32

Reading 5: Exodus 33–36

Reading 6: Exodus 37–40

IN METALLURGY, a science concerned with the behavior of metallic elements, *crushing* is one of the primary steps in mineral processing, preparing those minerals for future use by breaking their existing molecular structure. We humans, too, experience various forms of "crushing" on our way to realizing our higher purpose. Change is hard; transforming from one state of being to another can be painful, and no one willingly wants to experience pain. We often find our minds cluttered, insecurities present, and ourselves isolated from others.

Like the Israelites in Exodus, we have a tendency to turn away from God in these uncertain moments. We become uncomfortable and anxious. While our readings describe a distant time in history, we can relate to the experiences recounted. We run toward things God instructs us to avoid. We can run toward toxic relationships and bad habits that stunt our growth, and in the midst of being "crushed," we rush into more trouble, instead of trying to find a greater calling.

On the way to finding our new purpose, we need people praying for us, just as Moses did. When we make wrong turns, we need someone praying. When we deal with situations we never asked for, we need someone praying.

It takes work to get to the places God promised us, and God cares about every detail—even when it gets hard. God can show us the way, even in the form of a cloud. Look for your cloud in the crushing.

REFLECTION QUESTIONS

1. **Exodus 19–21:** In Exodus 20:8 we read, "Remember the Sabbath and treat it as holy." Why is the Sabbath so important?

2. **Exodus 22–25:** Why was instruction so important for the Israelites? How do you see God's instruction today?

3. **Exodus 26–29:** There are important symbols in Exodus, like the priest's chest pendant and the flower ornament. What items or symbols hold significance in your life and why?

4. **Exodus 30–32:** Moses intercedes on behalf of the Israelite people in Exodus 32:11. What does this tell you about God and Moses?

5. **Exodus 33–36:** In Exodus 35, we learn that everyone was eager to use their gifts, including the women. How do you use your gifts during difficult times?

6. **Exodus 37–40:** What do you think the cloud covering the temple in Exodus 40 represents?

POINTS TO PONDER

1. Think of a time you have experienced a form of crushing. How did you cope?
2. Looking back now, how has God used that time of crushing for you to learn and grow?
3. How can the lessons you have learned help you navigate future hardships?

ACTIVITY

It's never easy to get through hard moments in our lives, but if you are here today, you've taken another step. Take a few minutes to write down something you want to overcome on a loose piece of paper. Then crumple it up and throw it away. This symbolizes taking back your power and giving it to God.

GUIDED PRAYER

God, thank you that I am still here. Thank you for preparing me for my next steps toward walking in my destiny. Amen.

WEEK 5

I NEED WHAT YOU HAVE

READINGS

Reading 1: Matthew 1–3

Reading 2: Matthew 4–7

Reading 3: Matthew 8–11

Reading 4: Matthew 12–15

Reading 5: Matthew 16–19

Reading 6: Matthew 20–22

THE BOOK OF MATTHEW was written during the 1st century in a community under the rule of the Roman Empire. During this time, Jesus faced not only persecution but envy. The religious leaders throughout the book of Matthew saw the adoration and attention Jesus received and did not like it. They often wondered how a boy from Nazareth could know more than they did. They questioned his ability to heal (12:24) and even demanded additional signs from him to prove he was who he said he was (12:38). This is what envy can do. What they didn't see was Jesus's prayer life and the internal struggle he was experiencing. There may even have been other people watching in the distance thinking, "I want what you have."

It's easy for us, too, to have those thoughts in a social media age when we think we see everyone's path on the World Wide Web. This wasn't true for Jesus and is not the truth for many of us. In Matthew, we only see highlights of Jesus's ministry. But we are more than what people see, and the same is true for the sister next to you. You don't want what others have; you want what God has for *you*.

So, before you say or think you want what someone else has, take a minute, breathe, and remember, everything you already need is in you. Ask God to show you.

REFLECTION QUESTIONS

1. **Matthew 1–3:** How would you describe the faith of Mary and Joseph?

2. **Matthew 4–7:** What is something new you learned about the Sermon on the Mount reading these chapters?

3. **Matthew 8–11:** Which miracle in these chapters can you relate to the most and why?

4. **Matthew 12–15:** How do you think the man with the withered hand felt?

5. **Matthew 16–19:** What does Jesus teach his followers about forgiveness in Matthew 18?

6. **Matthew 20–22:** What do you learn from Jesus about love in these chapters?

POINTS TO PONDER

1. Why do we sometimes want what others have? Really think about it. When has this happened in your life?
2. We have to work on ourselves behind closed doors. What have you done to get closer to the person God has called you to be?
3. Have you asked and received? When you searched for God, what did you find?

ACTION OF THE WEEK

When was the last time you showcased your gifts to someone? It's perfectly fine to celebrate your talents from time to time. This week, consider sharing one of your skills or strengths with another person. This could be by offering your expertise in a situation, sharing an achievement that you are proud of, or teaching somebody a skill you possess.

GUIDED PRAYER

Dear God, help me see my light when I'm blinded and distracted. Help me see and focus on you. God, I thank you for my light. Amen.

WEEK 6

TEAR DOWN YOUR BARRIERS

READINGS

Reading 1: Matthew 23–25

Reading 2: Matthew 26–28

Reading 3: Leviticus 1–4

Reading 4: Leviticus 5–8

Reading 5: Leviticus 9–12

Reading 6: Leviticus 13–15

WHILE LIFE IS MUCH DIFFERENT now than it was in Moses's time, we still must be careful and mindful of the difference between a boundary and a barrier. I remember once I was upset with a friend, and instead of establishing boundaries, I cut her off with no real explanation. I am sure you, too, have shut people out of your life prematurely.

You see, a boundary can always be moved and shifted. Boundaries help us maintain strong relationships with the people in our lives and God. But if we're not careful, boundaries can become barriers, and it's hard to see God when we have barriers in the way. Barriers can force us to miss people and block our view of who they truly are and the issues they face. I created a barrier with my friend that neither she nor God could get through. Barriers can cause us to close God out of our lives, leading us to believe we have no one to count on. Barriers—whatever they look like for you—can force you to deny God.

We all block things in order to protect ourselves. But before you build walls around your heart, consider what barriers you can tear down to bring you closer to God.

REFLECTION QUESTIONS

1. **Matthew 23–25:** Jesus ridiculed legal experts who established unrealistic expectations. Why do you think it was so hard for these leaders to accept Jesus and his message?

2. **Matthew 26–28:** What does Matthew 26:36–39 reveal to you about prayer?

3. **Leviticus 1–4:** What do the instructions given to the Israelite community reveal about God?

4. **Leviticus 5–8:** Like Aaron and his sons, we can all be spiritually cleaned and renewed. How has God done this for you?

5. **Leviticus 9–12:** The priest initiation helps us see there are things we must do to hear from God clearly. Are there things you need to get rid of?

6. **Leviticus 13–15:** There are provisions described to improve the health of the Israelites. In what ways can you honor this by better taking care of your mind, body, and soul?

POINTS TO PONDER

1. We sometimes place barriers right in the middle of a breakthrough or our healing. Have you done this?
2. In Matthew 25, the parable of the 10 bridesmaids presents a story about being prepared. From this, we can learn something about barriers and our relationships with others. What lessons can you see here?
3. We find certain things detestable—things we should stay away from and never go back to. What won't you go back to?

ACTIVITY

Children often help us see things in a new way. Ask a child about an issue that has caused a roadblock in your life. Listen to their response. You may get what you need to see things in a new light. Take time to journal about the experience and your insights.

GUIDED PRAYER

Dear Holy One, help me release and tear down anything that blocks me from getting to you. Give me the instruction and help me remember Jesus, who shows me freedom. Amen.

WEEK 7

PROSPER AND BE HAPPY

READINGS

Reading 1: Psalms 1–3

Reading 2: Leviticus 16–19

Reading 3: Leviticus 20–23

Reading 4: Psalms 4–6

Reading 5: Leviticus 24–27

Reading 6: Psalms 7–10

I REMEMBER A TIME WHEN I wasn't happy. I was sad at work, became entrenched in gossip, believed what others said about me, and lost sight of God. I couldn't experience happiness until I focused and followed God's instructions. I began to speak life and positivity over situations. When someone would come to me with gossip, I would stop them and let them know I no longer wanted to talk about others. I turned to things that produced fruit and not confusion. As I continued to do this, prosperity came into my life and I began to grow.

We all experience unwanted situations, what the psalmist symbolizes with the image of "thousands of people surrounding me on all sides" (Psalm 3:6).

But a release can happen in the midst of tribulations, and obedience can lead to freedom and new understandings. Embrace your testimony and grab your happy. God has already crowned you with glory and grandeur (Psalm 8:5).

REFLECTION QUESTIONS

1. **Psalms 1–3:** Which verse in these chapters can help you in this season of your life?

2. **Leviticus 16–19:** What helped Aaron while he was grieving for his two sons?

____

____

3. **Psalms 4–6:** The Psalms express vulnerability. Is it hard for you to be vulnerable with others and God? Why or why not?

____

____

POINTS TO PONDER

1. Can happiness be forever, or is it temporary?
2. The book of Leviticus reminds us of how important it is to rest. What does rest look like for you?
3. The book of Psalms expresses the importance of worship and celebration. What does celebration look like for you?

ACTION OF THE WEEK

Psalms gives the Israelite people direction. How can you build on the Word of God to map out your own directions to happiness? Think of one thing you need to prosper, and commit to bringing this into your life during the week.

GUIDED PRAYER

Lord, like the psalmist, I rejoice in your salvation in the gates of Daughter Zion. I pray for your guidance as I navigate my daily happiness. Amen.

WEEK 8

THE BLESSING

READINGS

Reading 1: Numbers 1–4

Reading 2: Numbers 5–6

Reading 3: Proverbs 1–3

Reading 4: Numbers 7–9

Reading 5: Numbers 10–13

Reading 6: Proverbs 4–7

AS YOU DIG DEEPER into reading the Bible and grabbing the blessings God has for you, it's important to understand that one of God's greatest blessings is *you*. We can keep this in mind as we read certain passages from this week's scripture that describe codes and perspectives about women that seem far removed from our lives today. If you're like me, you may have wrestled with the readings, and this is fine. Sometimes we must wrestle with what we read to reach a deeper understanding and find the blessing.

Numbers continues the narrative of God's interaction with the Israelites as they pursue their complex journey to the promised land. Miriam, who was a leader and Moses's sister, experienced very unfortunate and rather unfair circumstances. The blessing of traveling to the promised land is shadowed not only by the disobedience of the Israelite community but also by the treatment Miriam received.

When people try to blame and mistreat us, when we're in a situation like Miriam's, let's remember *we* are a blessing. Go get your blessing and watch God work in the background.

REFLECTION QUESTIONS

1. **Numbers 1–4:** God spoke to Moses at different times and places. Where has God spoken to you lately?

2. **Numbers 5–6:** In Numbers 6:24–26, you can find a benediction recited by many churches. What is the importance of a benediction to you?

3. **Proverbs 1–3:** Reflecting on Proverbs 1:24, describe how we sometimes miss blessings because we don't pay attention.

4. **Numbers 7–9:** Numbers helps us see how blessings can come when we execute a vision. What is one of your missions in life?

5. **Numbers 10–13:** The Israelite people complain about waiting on their blessings. What does this teach us about trusting in God?

6. **Proverbs 4–7:** Proverbs 4:12 tells us, "When you walk, you won't be hindered; when you run, you won't stumble." What does this verse mean to you?

____

____

POINTS TO PONDER

1. Blessings point us to our next steps. How have your blessings directed your next steps?
2. What is the best advice you've received to keep going when times are tough?
3. If you could tell your younger self anything about blessings, what would you say?

VERSE OF THE WEEK

In Numbers 6:23–26, God gives a directive to Moses for Aaron and his sons. God tells them to pronounce this blessing: "The Lord bless you and protect you. The Lord make his face shine on you and be gracious to you. The Lord lift up his face to you and grant you peace." How can you receive this blessing in your own life?

GUIDED PRAYER

God, help me to believe and remember that I am the blessing. Help me lean on wisdom, trusting you every day I wake up. Amen.

WEEK 9

DELAY DOES NOT MEAN DENIAL

READINGS

Reading 1: Numbers 14–16

Reading 2: Numbers 17–19

Reading 3: Numbers 20–22

Reading 4: Proverbs 8–11

Reading 5: Numbers 23–26

Reading 6: Proverbs 12–14

I REMEMBER HEARING THE WORD "No" at what felt like one of the lowest points in my life. I felt defeated. If I knew then what I know now, the "No" wouldn't have been as devastating, because God never denied me anything. God simply said, "Not yet." Even when people tried to stop me, God was still preparing me for my next destination. Just like the Israelites, who complained in Numbers 14 about their current situation because they could not see that their delay was not a denial, we also experience twists and turns on our journeys. We all experience "No." We all see others accomplish things before we do. We all have felt isolated and unsure of what to do.

Truthfully, the middle of the delay is the hard part. In these moments of uncertainties, tests, and roadblocks, remember that God has a plan. Don't pull away from God's instructions; look around and see what you can learn. Even in our delay God speaks.

REFLECTION QUESTIONS

1. **Numbers 14–16:** In Numbers 14, the entire Israelite community is frustrated by their delay. What can you learn about faith in these chapters?

2. **Numbers 17–19:** What message do you see in Numbers 18 about being focused while waiting?

3. **Numbers 20–22:** In Numbers 20, Edom refuses to let Moses and the Israelite people cross through the land. What message do you see in this part of the story?

POINTS TO PONDER

1. We sometimes have the tendency to force things (Numbers 22:30–33). Do you force things in your life to work out?
2. What part of your life do you feel is being delayed? Why do you feel that way?
3. What is the best advice you ever received when you were sad about a delay?

ACTIVITY

Spend some time giving thanks and reverence to God. Find a quiet and comfortable place, play a song that inspires you, and spend ten minutes with God. Thank God for protection, and for patience in moments of waiting.

GUIDED PRAYER

God, you are true to your Word. Thank you for protecting me and preparing me for my next destination. Amen.

WEEK 10

I'M JUST A VESSEL

READINGS

Reading 1: Numbers 27–30

Reading 2: Numbers 31–33

Reading 3: Numbers 34–36

Reading 4: Mark 1–5

Reading 5: Mark 6–10

Reading 6: Mark 11–16

SOMETIMES, WE SAY "I'm just a vessel" to please others. We may even use this language to justify overworking or ill treatment. Sometimes, people watch us work hard and say, "God is pleased," and we go home unfulfilled. They see our work but not us.

In Numbers 27, Zelophehad's daughters—Mahlah, Noa, Hoglah, Milcah, and Tirzah—were five women who knew they were more than the eye could see. Today, they show us that we are more than what we do. We are more than what we've experienced. These women declared more for their lives even when they were overlooked and ignored. Yes, we can change laws like the daughters of Zelophehad. If we empty ourselves to depletion, we can't live.

Like physical vessels, we are so much more than what people see, and we deserve to be taken care of. We have to filter and drive out things that contaminate us. It reminds me of the saying, "I don't look like what I've been through." Never let others' negative ideas or treatment limit who you are and what you can achieve. We are more than *just* vessels—we hold the secrets of God's plan for this world.

REFLECTION QUESTIONS

1. **Numbers 27–30:** Why do you think God focuses on rest so often in these chapters?

2. **Numbers 31–33:** Why do you think God instructs the Israelite people to drive out all the inhabitants of the land?

3. **Numbers 34–36:** What did you learn about being a vessel for God from Zelophehad's daughters?

4. **Mark 1–5:** In Mark 3:21, why do you think Jesus's family says, "He's out of his mind"?

5. **Mark 6–10:** Many did not recognize Jesus as the Messiah or honor his divinity. How have people honored or dishonored your gifts?

6. **Mark 11–16:** Reflecting on Mark 15:21, how has this verse been used in relation to being a vessel for God? What other meanings do you see when reading this verse?

POINTS TO PONDER

1. What differences do you see in the books of Matthew and Mark?
2. The power of Zelophehad's daughters lives in us today, although unfortunately teamwork doesn't always work. Have you ever judged other people in your life? Did you refuse to see their light?
3. People will notice we are good at many things and request a lot from us. How have you experienced this, and how did you handle those requests?

ACTION OF THE WEEK

Reflect on your responses to this week's prompt about being a vessel for God. Reflect on how you can commit to putting this into action during the coming week.

GUIDED PRAYER

God, let me remember to take care of myself. Let me have enough energy to, like Mary Magdalene, give the report and help bring forth your works in the world. Amen.

WEEK 11

BEARING BURDENS

READINGS

Reading 1: Deuteronomy 1–4

Reading 2: Deuteronomy 5–8

Reading 3: Psalms 11–14

Reading 4: Deuteronomy 9–11

Reading 5: Deuteronomy 12–15

Reading 6: Psalms 15–17

IT'S HARD TO MOVE WITH A HEAVY LOAD on your back. After a long day, have you ever sat on the edge of your bed, burdened and exhausted, barely able to get your nightclothes on? Do you ever ask yourself, "What am I doing?" Sometimes, to help God remove burdens, we need reminders.

Sometimes, we place those burdens on ourselves. For me, the hardest burdens to unload were those I placed on myself. I said yes when I should have said no. I cared more about the success of a company than myself. I stayed connected too long to people who didn't care. I was bearing burdens never assigned to me. Learn from me—don't do this. You are not your burdens, and some burdens you should have never carried in the first place.

Sometimes, the burdens we bear are placed upon us, and we think we have to carry and figure them out alone, which is not true. When you forget and burdens feel too heavy for you to move, remember that God, "the one who gives you the strength to be prosperous in order to establish the covenant he made with your ancestors" (Deuteronomy 8:18), will help you carry them.

REFLECTION QUESTIONS

1. **Deuteronomy 1–4:** Reflect on Deuteronomy 2:7. Does this passage hold true for you?

2. **Deuteronomy 5–8:** What does it mean for you to love God with all your heart?

3. **Psalms 11–14:** Psalm 11:3 speaks of challenges when "the very bottom of things falls out." How do you lean on God in tough times?

4. **Deuteronomy 9–11:** Are there any instructions in this section that you can relate to?

5. **Deuteronomy 12–15:** What can you learn about bearing burdens from Deuteronomy 12:32?

6. **Psalms 15–17:** In Psalm 17:6, David pleads for God to hear his calls. How can we find comfort from God in the midst of fear?

POINTS TO PONDER

1. Have you ever had to transition out of a job or position? What did you do to help establish a smooth transfer of responsibilities?
2. When it's time to get going, we must have a lighter load. How can you lighten your load?
3. How have you held the people you love accountable for their actions?

ACTION OF THE WEEK

Take a few minutes to compose a psalm to God on a piece of paper. It can be of lament, questioning, or celebration. Feel free to be vulnerable and remember that God hears and answers our cries. Reflect on how you can carry the psalm with you in the week ahead.

GUIDED PRAYER

God, let me seek you with all my heart. Give me the wisdom and assistance to remove burdens that don't belong to me. Amen.

WEEK 12

BLESSED OR CURSED

READINGS

Reading 1: Deuteronomy 16–18

Reading 2: Deuteronomy 19–21

Reading 3: Psalms 18–21

Reading 4: Deuteronomy 22–25

Reading 5: Deuteronomy 26–28

Reading 6: Psalms 22–25

WHEN WE LIGHTEN OUR LOADS, we can receive and enjoy our blessings. Sometimes, blessings are right in front of us, and all we have to do is grab them. This can be hard when blessings feel more like curses. You know, when you have to move from an exciting city to a small town, or when you receive the job at a less well-known company. When opportunities don't look how we want them to, we sometimes ignore the blessing.

In Psalm 20:1 we read, "I pray that the Lord answers you whenever you are in trouble. Let the name of Jacob's God protect you." God can turn all that we believe to be curses into blessings. What others thought would bring us down can be for our good. After everything you've experienced, I'm so thankful you're still here. Truly, you are blessed—walk in it.

REFLECTION QUESTIONS

1. **Deuteronomy 19–21:** What lesson about blessings can you pull from Deuteronomy 20:20?

2. **Deuteronomy 22–25:** What does Deuteronomy 23 reveal to you about God turning "curses" into blessings?

3. **Psalms 22–25:** What does Psalm 25 teach us about the power of prayer during difficult times?

POINTS TO PONDER

1. It's always best to listen to God. Have you ever intentionally ignored God's voice? Why? What was this experience like?
2. Have you ever stopped reading a book because it hit too close to home? Did you have this moment during this week's readings?
3. When has God turned a situation around for your good? Did this change the way you think about your life?

ACTIVITY

We should treat people the way we want to be treated and protect what the Lord has given us. As women, we may not always experience appropriate treatment from others. Think about how you want others to treat you, and think of a short statement that sums up your thought. Carry this thought with you during the week.

GUIDED PRAYER

God, my rock, open my eyes to see gifts from you. Give me the courage, wisdom, and instruction to grab my blessings when it's time. Amen.

WEEK 13

YOUR OWN JORDAN RIVER

READINGS

Reading 1: Deuteronomy 29–31

Reading 2: Deuteronomy 32–34

Reading 3: Joshua 1–4

Reading 4: Joshua 5–8

Reading 5: Joshua 9–12

Reading 6: Joshua 13–16

WE ALL HAVE OUR OWN JORDAN RIVER. Like the Israelites in Joshua 3, we face hardships and calamities and are given opportunities to cross over into something new. On our journeys, when we encounter a dangerous crossing, we may pause and even feel afraid. One must remember what's needed to cross our Jordan Rivers.

In order to cross *over*, we need a captain we trust and to remember to trust God. Oftentimes our captains have been walking alongside us all our lives. They are people who believed in us before we believed in ourselves. I don't know about you, but you won't catch me crossing a river with people I have no confidence in. I need my Rahab: someone who takes action in the midst of danger, who holds our hands even as they are also crossing their own Jordan River.

When we encounter these moments, we can lose faith and turn around or we can remember to trust in God and forge ahead. God can prepare everything around us so we are successful in our difficult tasks. God fights for us. So, cross over to dry land. God is waiting for you.

REFLECTION QUESTIONS

1. **Deuteronomy 29–31:** In Deuteronomy 29, Moses reminds Israel about what God has done for them. If Moses summoned you, what would he remind you that God has done for you in the last year?

2. **Deuteronomy 32–34:** What is your favorite line in Moses's poem found in Deuteronomy 32 and why?

3. **Joshua 1–4:** What type of character is Rahab in the Israelite story? Why is she important?

4. **Joshua 5–8:** In Joshua 5, the commander of heavenly hosts tells Joshua to take off his sandals for he is on holy ground. Holy ground can be where we commune with God. What's your holy ground?

5. **Joshua 9–12:** In Joshua 9, the Israelites learn they have been deceived. How do you deal with deception?

6. **Joshua 13–16:** In Joshua 15:18, Caleb asks Achsah, "What can I do for you?" (NIV) What do you want for your own life right now?

____

____

POINTS TO PONDER

1. Who do you trust to help you cross your own Jordan River? Oftentimes these people are in the background and overlooked.
2. What are some victories you have experienced in recent times?
3. What have you learned about yourself as you crossed your own Jordan River?

ACTIVITY

Sometimes we forget the rivers God has brought us over. This activity helps you remember and encourages you to keep going. Find some colored pens or pencils and some drawing paper, and let your creativity run free!

1. Think about the rivers you've had in your life from childhood until present.
2. Reflect on what or who helped you over your rivers.
3. Take some time to draw your rivers. Your river can look like whatever feels authentic. Also feel free to use words, including people, places, and memories.
4. Take time to reflect on your drawing.

GUIDED PRAYER

Oh Holy One, when I get to my rivers, help me cross over to dry land. Send the people, tools, and resources I will need to make it over. Amen.

WEEK 14

I AM A WINNER!

READINGS

Reading 1: Joshua 17–20

Reading 2: Joshua 21–24

Reading 3: Proverbs 15–17

Reading 4: Judges 1–3

Reading 5: Judges 4–6

Reading 6: Judges 7–10

CONFIDENCE COMES IN MANY FORMS and is needed to be successful. It allows us to keep going even when we think we have failed. And, if we're honest, meeting a confident woman can make others uncomfortable. Sometimes her confidence is questioned, challenged, and even stigmatized. There have been times people would tell me, "You're just too confident," or they'd say things to make me question myself. Maybe this has happened to you, and you started to think you weren't a winner.

In Judges 4, we encounter for the first time a woman judge, Deborah. Deborah and Jael work together and, within their social definition, win. What I admire about Deborah is that she knew she was a winner before she even faced the battle. Her actions and language exuded confidence and faith in God.

You have to confidently tell yourself "I am a winner" before putting yourself out there. Sometimes, we've already won before we realize it. Most importantly, we can't win alone, and we shouldn't try to. We can lean on God, not letting the world's definition of winning distract us. Believe you've got this with God's help, walk in confidence, and keep winning!

REFLECTION QUESTIONS

1. **Joshua 17–20:** In Joshua 17, how do the daughters of Zelophehad protect what God gave them?

2. **Joshua 21–24:** How does God ordain the Levites to be taken care of by the larger people of Israel?

3. **Proverbs 15–17:** Proverbs 16:2 says, "All the ways of people are pure in their eyes, but the Lord tests the motives." How can you connect this verse to being a winner?

4. **Judges 1–3:** In Judges 2, a whole generation is unaware of what the Lord did for their ancestors. How have you seen this in the world?

5. **Judges 4–6:** What can you learn from Gideon about winning?

6. **Judges 7–10:** Abimelech hired reckless men (Judges 9:4) and destruction followed. Have you ever engaged with someone you shouldn't have? What did you learn?

POINTS TO PONDER

1. Sometimes, winning is not a physical prize but one we walk away with in our minds and hearts. What is a spiritual winning you received?
2. What did you learn from Deborah about winning?
3. You may not feel the glory of the win today, but it's coming. What wins are you looking forward to?

ACTION OF THE WEEK

It's easy to fall into the ways of the world and society's idea of "winning." Reflect on this verse from Proverbs 16:2: "All the ways of people are pure in their eyes, but the Lord tests the motives." This week, bring to mind this passage with every decision you make, and think about your motives. Do they serve you or God? Take time to write down your thoughts.

GUIDED PRAYER

God, I declare that wherever I go and whatever I do, I am a winner. Lead and guide me to walk in my victory with confidence and integrity. Amen.

WEEK 15

TRUST GOD'S TRACK RECORD

READINGS

Reading 1: Judges 11–14

Reading 2: Judges 15–17

Reading 3: Judges 18–21

Reading 4: Psalms 26–29

Reading 5: Psalms 30–33

Reading 6: Psalms 34–37

ALLYSON FELIX IS NOW THE MOST DECORATED American athlete in track and field Olympic history. After she had a baby, many counted her out, but with persistence, determination, and talent, she proved God right and everyone who doubted her wrong. No one can take her accomplishments away; her track record is the proof. God also has a remarkable record. God continuously directed and kept promises to the people of Israel. He released them from the power of Pharaoh and provided a way in the wilderness. While they disobeyed God, God continuously rescued them from destruction.

Tracking God's record is easy. It gets difficult when we confuse our records with God's. We can make choices and decisions far from God and believe they were God's doing. We begin to believe everything we are experiencing is because of God and take no accountability. Our choices sometimes don't reflect what God has done for us.

Trusting God allows God to find openings for his will to be done on Earth. When you are faced with trying times and you feel like giving up, trust God's track record. God is searching for who will be obedient. Like Allyson's record, God's record is signed, sealed, and delivered. So, keep your eyes on God and trust God's unbeatable record.

REFLECTION QUESTIONS

1. **Judges 11–14:** What does Jephthah's story reveal to you about God's track record?

2. **Judges 15–17:** What could Samson have done differently in his dealings with women?

3. **Judges 18–21:** The owner of the house in Judges 19:20 wanted to help, but it did not end well. Can you relate to this?

4. **Psalms 26–29:** The book of Psalms shows us that God can handle our questions. What questions do you have for God at this time in your life?

5. **Psalms 30–33:** Which psalm resonates with you the most and why?

6. **Psalms 34–37:** Which psalm would you read to encourage women who suffer like those in this week's readings do?

____

____

POINTS TO PONDER

1. What has God promised you that has come to pass?
2. What do people usually put on God's track record that doesn't belong there? Think of some of the realities of the women in the readings this week.
3. When people look over your track record, what do you want to be on it?

VERSE OF THE WEEK

Reflect on what the following verse means to you: "That's why all the faithful should pray to you during troubled times, so that a great flood of water won't reach them. You are my secret hideout! You protect me from trouble. You surround me with songs of rescue! I will instruct you and teach you about the direction you should go. I'll advise you and keep my eye on you" (Psalms 32:6–8).

GUIDED PRAYER

God, you have the perfect track record. Help me remember and walk in confidence that you, God, have already won the race for me. Amen.

WEEK 16

STOP STRESSING AND START PRAYING

READINGS

Reading 1: Ruth 1–4

Reading 2: 1 Samuel 1–3

Reading 3: 1 Samuel 4–7

Reading 4: 1 Samuel 8–11

Reading 5: 1 Samuel 12–14

Reading 6: 1 Samuel 15–17

THE PEOPLE IN OUR READINGS this week experienced a lot of stressful situations. In Ruth 1, we learn that stress can lead us to push loved ones away and even forget our own name. Naomi was grieving the death of her husband and two sons, and she was not sure where to go or what to do. We even learn how stress can alter our diets from Hannah (1 Samuel 1), as she was distraught because of how she was being treated and wanting to have a child. Like these women, we also have experienced the symptoms of stress.

The phrase "just pray about it" can seem cliché to those who continuously receive the short end of the stick. There are no excuses for the social pressures and realities Hannah, Naomi, and Ruth had to deal with. No one should have to worry about where their next meal will come from. But we, like them, have to find a way to live. Their journeys looked different, and yet prayer and praise to God was present. In order to be released, we need to pray.

Even when we face our Goliaths, be sure to pray. God's answer may not always come in the form we want, but an answer will come. Be wise: stop stressful situations before they take up space in your mind and body. Stop stress in its tracks and thank God for the strength to do this every time.

REFLECTION QUESTIONS

1. **Ruth 1–4:** What did you learn from Naomi, Ruth, and Orpah's relationship?

2. **1 Samuel 1–3:** The Lord paid attention to Hannah, and she gave birth to three sons and two daughters. When has God provided for you?

3. **1 Samuel 4–7:** What is the significance of the Ark of the Lord?

4. **1 Samuel 8–11:** What can you learn from Samuel about prayer?

5. **1 Samuel 12–14:** In 1 Samuel 13, Saul panicked after hearing from God. Have you panicked and made hasty decisions without hearing and listening to God? What did you learn?

6. **1 Samuel 15–17:** 1 Samuel 15:22 teaches us to pay attention and obey. What does this verse mean to you?

____

____

POINTS TO PONDER

1. Naomi became the godmother to Ruth's child. This is a prayer being answered in an unexpected way. Consider how God has answered your prayers in unexpected ways.
2. Hiding who we are can be stressful. Have you ever concealed who you are? (1 Samuel 10:23)
3. God may not answer our prayers the same day we pray. Have you experienced God answering a prayer months or even years later?

ACTIVITY

We are human and we all will experience stress, but we are able to find ways to not just cope but to live intentionally. Take a moment to listen to your body—are you tense?—and create a prayer that reflects what you want out of this week to make self-care a priority.

GUIDED PRAYER

Dear God, help me relax and lean on you. Help me live without stress and fear. Help me get closer to you. Amen.

WEEK 17

MOVING THE ARK

READINGS

Reading 1: 1 Samuel 18–21

Reading 2: 1 Samuel 22–25

Reading 3: 1 Samuel 26–29

Reading 4: 1 Samuel 30–31

Reading 5: 2 Samuel 1–4

Reading 6: 2 Samuel 5–8

AS DAVID AND OTHERS PREPARED THE ARK, God had already given instructions, but they were unable to execute them. The ark was very important to God, as are we. Not listening to God and skipping instructions can lead to uneasy feelings, like doubt and remorse, and unfortunate circumstances. We can find ourselves upset and wondering why we are experiencing these feelings and not moving on. We have to remember not to cut corners and leave God out of our plans. In the end, doing this only cheats ourselves. As we move our arks, God cares about the details, and we should, too. Follow God's instructions and see the many arks you can successfully move.

REFLECTION QUESTIONS

1. **1 Samuel 22–25:** Reread the beginning of 1 Samuel 22. Why was David able to survive?

2. **1 Samuel 26–29:** Saul dealt with insecurities. Why do you think it was so hard for Saul to focus on David and not his relationship with God?

3. **2 Samuel 5–8:** Why do you think Michal lost respect for David in 2 Samuel 6?

POINTS TO PONDER

1. Jealousy can feel like an ark. We can store up heavy feelings inside of ourselves. How have you removed these feelings of insecurity?
2. Everyone plays a role in moving the Ark (1 Samuel 30:22–25). Has your role ever been overlooked? How did you handle this?
3. Have you ever been working in a group and others refused to listen to God? What was the outcome? If faced with this situation, what would you do?

VERSE OF THE WEEK

Reflect on 2 Samuel 22:32–33: "Now really, who is divine except the Lord? And who is a rock except our God? Only God! My mighty fortress, who makes my way perfect." How do these words play out in your life?

GUIDED PRAYER

Holy One, thank you for instructing me. Give me the will and determination to follow your instructions until the end of my life. Amen.

WEEK 18

GOD HAS NOT FORGOTTEN

READINGS

Reading 1: 2 Samuel 9–12

Reading 2: 2 Samuel 13–15

Reading 3: 2 Samuel 16–18

Reading 4: 2 Samuel 19–21

Reading 5: 2 Samuel 22–24

Reading 6: Psalms 38–41

I REMEMBER WHEN I THOUGHT GOD FORGOT ABOUT ME. I felt like I couldn't hear God, and every time I turned around it seemed like someone else was accomplishing a goal while I wasn't. But it wasn't that God forgot about me—I simply forgot who God is. We are human; from our limited perspective, it can seem like everyone but us receives what they prayed for.

Biblical figures had this experience, too. Mephibosheth lost his father at a young age and, in the ensuing chaos, lost the use of his legs, too. He had to wait years before taking his rightful place. He went through childhood and his teenage years probably thinking God forgot about him, and if we are honest, we can also think God has forgotten about us. But when we get to these places on our journeys, God always sends a sign—a reminder that we are not forgotten. For Mephibosheth, it was David. For me, it was my Nana. She had a way of sensing discouragement and would remind me of how God has kept me by saying, "God will take care of you." This simple response was the exact confirmation I needed.

Whatever you are in need of, whatever you are praying for, have confidence that God has not forgotten you. Just be ready when it's your turn.

REFLECTION QUESTIONS

1. **2 Samuel 9–12:** How does the story of David and Mephibosheth help us see God's love in our lives?

2. **2 Samuel 13–15:** How do you think Tamar felt? Do you think she believed God remembered her?

3. **2 Samuel 16–18:** The story of Absalom shows us to take care when seeking advice. Have you ever been misdirected when you were looking for comfort?

4. **2 Samuel 19–21:** Joab encouraged the king to do right by those who loved him. Who holds you accountable to God?

5. **2 Samuel 22–24:** What line in David's song of praise can you relate to in this moment of your life?

6. **Psalms 38–41:** What is the hardest part about waiting for God? Find a verse to support your answer within these chapters.

POINTS TO PONDER

1. When have you felt forgotten by God?
2. Sometimes, God is ready to guide us to our next destination, but we haven't done the work. How do you prepare for God?
3. What is the difference between forgetting and forgiving?

VERSE OF THE WEEK

Consider what this verse means to you: "He lifted me out of the pit of death, out of the mud and filth, and set my feet on solid rock. He steadied my legs. He put a new song in my mouth, a song of praise for our God. Many people will learn of this and be amazed; they will trust the Lord" (Psalm 40:2–3).

GUIDED PRAYER

Gracious God, thank you for never forgetting me. Help me be ready for you when it's my time to move to my next destination. Amen.

WEEK 19

THE DROUGHT IS ALMOST OVER

READINGS

Reading 1: 1 Kings 1–4

Reading 2: 1 Kings 5–7

Reading 3: 1 Kings 8–10

Reading 4: 1 Kings 11–14

Reading 5: 1 Kings 15–18

Reading 6: 1 Kings 19–22

HAVE YOU EVER REQUESTED WATER AT A RESTAURANT and after a few minutes wondered where the waiter was with your drink? The restaurant is clearly busy, but this doesn't help your thirst and your need of water. The waiter walks past the table and informs you the water is on the way. While your thirst is not quenched, there is relief in knowing the water will soon come. We also need this reassurance in our times of drought. A drought in our lives is not necessarily physical. A drought can happen in any season on any day.

In 1 Kings, Elijah prophesied a drought would take over the land for three years. Many of us can relate to the experience of weathering a long, hot drought. Sometimes it takes years for us to feel like our thirst is quenched. We can learn a lot about ourselves and who we are connected to in these moments. What we should remember is God's promise. When you're in the midst of a drought—physical or not—trust that water is coming your way. In 1 Kings 17:13–16, the widow at Zarephath and Elijah were experiencing a drought, and God made a way out of no way. Be encouraged to know droughts don't last forever. Even when rivers dry up, God still can move things around to quench our thirst.

REFLECTION QUESTIONS

1. **1 Kings 1–4:** David's health was deteriorating, and he needed help. When has God sent you help when you needed it?

2. **1 Kings 5–7:** What does the meticulous detail involved in preparing and building the temple say to you?

3. **1 Kings 8–10:** Note some highlights from Solomon's prayer of dedication for the temple. What does the prayer convey to you about the temple's purpose?

4. **1 Kings 11–14:** When things seem to be going right, we can become lax in our prayer and obedience like Rehoboam. Has this ever happened to you?

5. **1 Kings 15–18:** What did you learn from Elijah and the widow of Zarephath?

6. **1 Kings 19–22:** God provided for Elijah even in a drought. How would you describe your faith in periods of drought in your life?

POINTS TO PONDER

1. God can provide both during the drought and after. Have you experienced God providing for you when you didn't know where the means would come from?
2. Have you ever connected with someone when you were both going through a hard time? How did this help your process?
3. Like he did for the widow from Zarephath (1 Kings 17:13–16), God can provide for us, too. How can you better trust that God will provide for you?

ACTION OF THE WEEK

Drought periods do not last forever, and there is always something we can learn from each other to make it through. On a piece of paper, spend a few minutes writing down three drought periods in your life and three lessons you can take from them. Post your lessons in a place you can see them (like sticky notes on a mirror) to inspire you throughout the week.

GUIDED PRAYER

Dear God, I pray I pay attention to your signs. Help me always seek you even in times of drought. Thank you for being the water that never runs dry. Amen.

WEEK 20

BOUNCING BACK

READINGS

Reading 1: 2 Kings 1–3

Reading 2: 2 Kings 4–7

Reading 3: 2 Kings 8–11

Reading 4: 2 Kings 12–15

Reading 5: 2 Kings 16–18

Reading 6: 2 Kings 19–22

AFTER I GRADUATED UNDERGRAD, I worked at a job where I wasn't happy. Around this same time my grandfather, who was my best friend, passed away. I was unfulfilled at my job and was experiencing my first heartbreak. I just couldn't find my fight. As time passed, I was able to make the best out of my situation, but it wasn't easy. It took me almost two years to find my balance and feel like myself again.

Every day I intentionally did something to help clear my mind and embrace my fire. I would listen to inspirational music, interviews, and sermons. I would send an email, make a call, or talk to someone to help me reach my goals. One step at a time, I was able to bounce back with God's help and direction.

We can think that nothing will happen to help us and can give up too early. Being connected to God is the ultimate way to bounce back, so stay connected to the source. The faithful woman in 2 Kings who received her possessions after years of hardships is our proof. After seven years of hardships, wondering, faithfulness, and discouragement, everything she had lost was restored. We don't always know when it will happen, but the good news is . . . it will happen. We bounce back to go forward. All we can do is what is required by the Lord.

REFLECTION QUESTIONS

1. **2 Kings 1–3:** Why do you think Elisha's request was honored by God in 2 Kings 2?

2. **2 Kings 4–7:** How would you describe the widow's situation and faith?

3. **2 Kings 8–11:** How did the Shunammite bounce back?

4. **2 Kings 12–15:** God hears Jehoahaz's prayer and helps the Israelites in 2 Kings 13. When was the last time you felt God's protection from danger?

5. **2 Kings 16–18:** What do these chapters teach us about respect?

6. **2 Kings 19–22:** The people and rulers refused to fully do what God required. Do you know what God requires of you?

POINTS TO PONDER

1. God has a way of maneuvering things around to assist in our bounce back. Sometimes we never know what is happening in the background. Have you ever found out more people were involved in your bounce back than you initially thought?
2. How have you walked alongside someone who needed a hand?
3. We all lose our way and need spiritual direction. Are you connected to spiritual groups, churches, or communities? How do these spaces help you?

VERSE OF THE WEEK

In 2 Kings 20:5, God sends a message to Isaiah: "I have heard your prayer and have seen your tears. So now I'm going to heal you." How can you relate this verse to the ways in which you have bounced back in your own life?

GUIDED PRAYER

Holy One, I pray for my bounce back. God give me the strength and ability to get back to who you created me to be. Amen.

WEEK 21

CAN YOU PASS THE TEST?

READINGS

Reading 1: 2 Kings 23–25

Reading 2: Luke 1–4

Reading 3: Luke 5–7

Reading 4: Luke 8–11

Reading 5: Luke 12–14

Reading 6: Luke 15–18

IN LUKE 5, JESUS CALLS HIS FIRST DISCIPLES. Jesus tells Simon, "Put out into deep water, and let down the nets for a catch" (NIV). Before this, Simon was trying to catch fish all night, but nothing seemed to work. I am sure he was tired and ready to go home, but he listened to Jesus and dropped his net into the water. He "caught such a large number of fish that their nets began to break" (Luke 5:6 NIV). This was a test, and it appears Simon passed.

Tests come in many forms. We often don't know when we're being tested. God is not seeing who is the best or quickest, but who will listen, who can withstand the questions. God's exams are not like what we experience in school. God is testing for comprehension—and it's always hard to pass a test with no faith.

The next time you find yourself undone by the challenges of life, listen closely to God and draw the hope and courage your faith provides. You can pass the test—just keep walking.

REFLECTION QUESTIONS

1. **2 Kings 23–25:** Why was it important for Josiah to take down anything that did not belong to God?

2. **Luke 1–4:** In Luke 1:64, the angels tell Zechariah what to name his son. He obeys and is able to speak again. When has God showed you that you passed a test in life?

3. **Luke 5–7:** Sometimes tests come in the form of breaking rules that harm others. Have you experienced this?

4. **Luke 8–11:** Why do you think Herod was confused?

5. **Luke 12–14:** Jesus questions the intentions of the leaders who are unwilling to help a woman bound by Satan. What are your intentions when helping others?

6. **Luke 15–18:** What does the parable of the lost sheep mean to you?

____

____

POINTS TO PONDER

1. Each time you face a test, you gain more confidence. What have you gained over the last year? How do you see yourself improving in making choices?
2. In Luke 10:27, Jesus says, "You must love the Lord your God with all your heart . . . and love your neighbor as yourself." Have you ever been tested to treat someone right and failed?
3. Tests help us produce good fruit (Luke 3:9). When have you been able to see this after going through a test?

ACTIVITY

In Luke 7:44–47, we are reintroduced to the woman with the alabaster jar. She used something of value to her, perfume, to anoint Jesus. Consider a time you have given up something valuable in service of something greater. Spend a few minutes to reflect on what you gained from your experience.

GUIDED PRAYER

Oh Holy God, help me prepare and have faith in you. Let me see the test and trust you can give me what I need to understand. Amen.

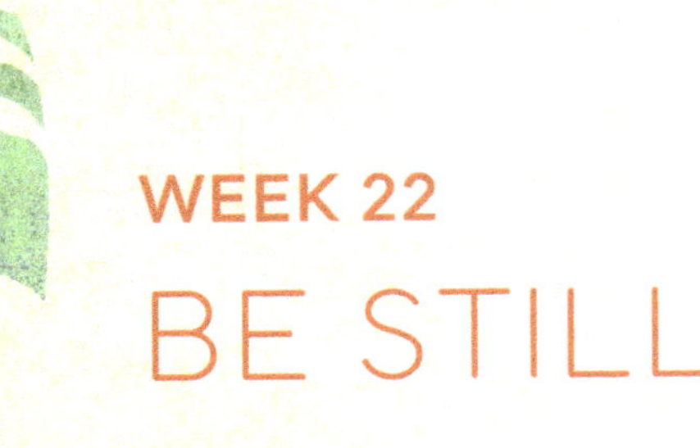

WEEK 22
BE STILL

READINGS

Reading 1: Luke 19–21

Reading 2: Luke 22–24

Reading 3: Psalms 42–47

Reading 4: Psalms 48–54

Reading 5: Psalms 55–61

Reading 6: Psalms 62–67

PSALM 46 IS A SONG for the descendants of Korah. It offers them hope as they encourage each other to keep trusting in God, even in the midst of tough times. In Psalm 46:10, they receive the message, "Be still, and know that I am God" (NLT). Being still is a practice, not just for the moment. Being still can literally protect us from hurt, harm, and danger. This practice allows us to hear from God and engage with people better. Although there are many benefits of being still, it can be difficult.

It's hard to be still when our current circumstances feel draining, the future is unpredictable, our goals seem unattainable, and the world just keeps moving. Honestly, being "on the go" is often honored, and slowing down is frowned upon. We have to find ways to listen to God and not how the world says we should move. There are certain things we can only hear when we are still. We can be guided and God's mysterious ways revealed. We, like the writer of this week's Psalms, can't escape the troubles of the world, but what we can do is find time to be still, wait, and listen for God's instructions.

This week, intentionally be still before speaking or acting. Write down what happened in and after the moment. See what you can learn. See what you can hear from God. Be still.

REFLECTION QUESTIONS

1. **Luke 19–21:** Luke 21:19 states, "By holding fast, you will gain your lives." What does this verse mean to you?

2. **Luke 22–24:** Peter denied Jesus publicly three times. What role did weakness and fear play in these moments?

3. **Psalms 42–47:** These psalms describe how God can sustain us in times of trouble. What hope does this provide you in your life now?

4. **Psalms 48–54:** The psalmist in Psalm 49 compels the reader to listen closely and pay attention. How can you do this in your life?

5. **Psalms 55–61:** Which of these psalms would you share with someone who is ready to give up?

6. **Psalms 62–67:** What do we learn about the characteristics of God in these chapters?

POINTS TO PONDER

1. The psalmist in Psalm 55:2 is desperate and is surrounded by violence: "Pay attention! Answer me! I can't sit still while complaining. I'm beside myself." Have you ever felt like this?
2. What advice would you give the psalmist?
3. When is it hard to be still? How have you worked on this?

ACTION OF THE WEEK

Psalm 46:10 reads, "Be still, and know that I am God." When you feel the urge to act in haste this week, challenge yourself to be still and trust God.

GUIDED PRAYER

Oh Holy One, I pray for the wisdom and obedience to know when to move and when to be still. Guide me and provide me with the tools to listen and trust you. Amen.

WEEK 23

GOD'S WAY IS THE RIGHT WAY

READINGS

Reading 1: 1 Chronicles 1–4

Reading 2: 1 Chronicles 5–8

Reading 3: 1 Chronicles 9–12

Reading 4: 1 Chronicles 13–16

Reading 5: 1 Chronicles 17–19

Reading 6: 1 Chronicles 20–22

SOMETIMES, WE HAVE TO GO BACK in order to see God's way. 1 Chronicles takes us down an ancestral history and timeline of events. We are shown God's work throughout generations and the bringing back together of people who strayed apart.

Like the people in our readings, we also get lost. We exile ourselves from God's protection and are desperate for lifelines. Hallelujah, there is good news for those of us who stray. We can always be "restored" and placed right back on track. Appreciate the way God redirects us when we don't listen. Appreciate the love that helps us see the way, because God's way is always the right way.

REFLECTION QUESTIONS

1. **1 Chronicles 9–12:** These readings tell us of the responsibilities of each tribe. What do you learn about God and teamwork?

---

2. **1 Chronicles 17–19:** How can you relate to David's prayer?

---

3. **1 Chronicles 20–22:** Why does God have a change of mind in 1 Chronicles 21:15?

POINTS TO PONDER

1. Have you ever made a decision you weren't sure about, choosing to go with what other people thought was the right thing to do?
2. It can be hard to actually know which way is God's way. What helps you discern which way to go?
3. What part of this week's readings helps you better discern God's way?

ACTIVITY

The long arc of history has a way of showing us God's movement. Bring to mind a moment from history that you find particularly inspiring or momentous and how you think God moved during that time. Take a few minutes to reflect on an inspiring moment in your own life history, too. In what ways do you think God was moving at that time?

GUIDED PRAYER

Oh Holy One! Thank you for showing me the way. Let the heavenly forces be with me as I make every decision. I pray for your grace and direction. Amen.

WEEK 24

IT'S PRAYING TIME

READINGS

Reading 1: 1 Chronicles 23–26

Reading 2: 1 Chronicles 27–29

Reading 3: 2 Chronicles 1–3

Reading 4: 2 Chronicles 4–7

Reading 5: 2 Chronicles 8–10

Reading 6: 2 Chronicles 11–13

BOLD WOMEN OF GOD, sometimes all we can do is pray. When nothing seems to be working, when we experience health issues, when we have turmoil in our families, when things just feel . . . bad, it's praying time!

In 1 Chronicles, we see people organizing to find their way back to God. Regardless of how the people were instructed, they had to pray. It's important to see that despite any amount of organization or what was faced, prayer was not only important but primary. You can cross every T and dot every I, but without prayer, moving forward will always feel harder than necessary.

When we mess up or confusion sets in, we can forget and turn away from God—so it's praying time! In 2 Chronicles 12, Rehoboam was a king who gained power and then turned away from God. We see someone who messed up, prayed, and had his request granted by God. As women, our process may not seem that easy. Although we are often exposed to gender inequalities and assumptions men don't experience, our endings can be glorious.

Even when we feel like we've exiled ourselves from God and our current realities exhaust us, prayer can help us focus. We can't get to God's heart without prayer. It's praying time!

REFLECTION QUESTIONS

1. **1 Chronicles 23–26:** The Levites were in charge of priestly duties and spiritual direction. When it's time to pray, which community or people in your life do you turn to?

2. **1 Chronicles 27–29:** A portion of 1 Chronicles 28:9 reads, "If you seek [God], he will be found by you." When has this happened for you lately?

3. **2 Chronicles 1–3:** Solomon first meets God in 2 Chronicles 1. When did you first meet God?

4. **2 Chronicles 4–7:** What have you learned about Solomon?

5. **2 Chronicles 8–10:** What can you assume about the Queen of Sheba and her power?

6. **2 Chronicles 11–13:** What consequences does Rehoboam face for abandoning the ways of God?

POINTS TO PONDER

1. David was honest, vulnerable, and relatable in his prayers to God. Are there any misconceptions you were taught about prayer?
2. How do you engage with God now? Are you comfortable being vulnerable during prayer time?
3. We often can be led astray and away from God. We begin to lean on the advice of those far away from God. Have you experienced this and found it hard to pray?

ACTIVITY

Many feel like prayer doesn't work because their situations don't change. What would you say to someone who did not realize it was time to pray? What wisdom, comfort, or inspiration would you include in your pitch?

GUIDED PRAYER

God, I need you. May my eyes be open to know I can always talk to you. I believe you hear this prayer just like you did for those before me. Amen.

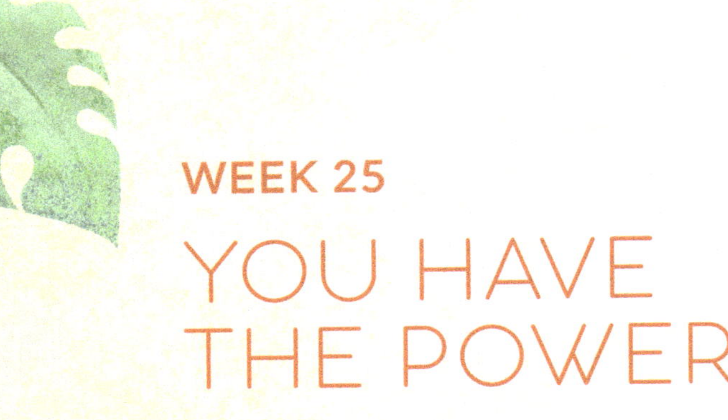

WEEK 25

YOU HAVE THE POWER

READINGS

Reading 1: Proverbs 18–21

Reading 2: Proverbs 22–24

Reading 3: Proverbs 25–27

Reading 4: Proverbs 28–31

Reading 5: 2 Chronicles 14–16

Reading 6: 2 Chronicles 17–19

HAVE YOU EVER FELT POWERLESS? I have. But God has already given us the power. Honestly, it just takes us a while to realize it. So much can interfere with how we see ourselves—from embracing what's inside of us. We read, see, internalize, and grow into ideas that limit us. We hide our power, hoping to be accepted by friends, strangers, family, and co-workers. We hide our power by accepting less than what we deserve. We have the power, but often we give it up.

As we will read in 1 Corinthians 4:20, "For the kingdom of God does not consist in talk but in power" (ESV). We must believe in the power of God and in the power God gives us. There are no words that hold more power than what God has instilled in you. Once I believed in my power, I was able to see God in a different way.

Every day you gain the power to be who you are, to live out your purpose, and to stick up for yourself. The world is God's, and we have the power to experience it in its fullness. Remember: "We also pray that you will be strengthened with all God's glorious power so you will have all the endurance and patience you need. May you be filled with joy" (Colossians 1:11, NLT).

REFLECTION QUESTIONS

1. **Proverbs 18–21:** Proverbs 18:6 centers on the importance of our words. When have you said unwise words? What would you say differently now?

2. **Proverbs 22–24:** What does Proverbs 23:23 mean to you?

3. **Proverbs 25–27:** What lesson can you pull from Proverbs 25:8 about power?

4. **Proverbs 28–31:** Proverbs 28:1 states, "The wicked flee though no one pursues, but the righteous are as bold as a lion." How does your faith empower you?

5. **2 Chronicles 14–16:** What lesson do we learn when Asa seeks help only from doctors?

6. **2 Chronicles 17–19:** Which of the reforms Jehoshaphat makes in 2 Chronicles 19 do you admire the most and why?

____

____

POINTS TO PONDER

1. Power is not in possession but in purpose. Is this completely true for you? Why or why not? (Proverbs 27:24)
2. Power is not just what we say, but also what we think. What negative thoughts can you change to help you realize your power?
3. Proverbs 29:11 states, "A fool gives full vent to his anger, but a wise man quietly holds it back" (RSV). Is this considered powerful today? Should there be a balance?

ACTION OF THE WEEK

Realizing our power is freeing. Take your power back! Think of a way that you can regain your power in the coming week. Create a statement that sums up your plan, then pronounce it out loud. Example: "This week I plan to speak up for myself and take my power back." Let this declaration strengthen you as you move throughout your week.

GUIDED PRAYER

God, help us see our power. We take back the power the world tried to take from us. Thank you for your help and guidance living in this world. Amen.

WEEK 26

WE'RE BETTER TOGETHER

READINGS

Reading 1: 2 Chronicles 20–24

Reading 2: 2 Chronicles 25–28

Reading 3: 2 Chronicles 29–32

Reading 4: 2 Chronicles 33–36

Reading 5: Psalms 68–72

Reading 6: Psalms 73–78

IT'S NOT ALWAYS EASY UNITING WITH OTHER WOMEN. We come from different places, backgrounds, cultures, and experiences. This is true for us and for those we read about in 2 Chronicles. Our differences make the world interesting. Our differences allow us to learn from each other. Coming together has its challenges, but when we learn to actually see and embrace one another, we are so much better together.

In 2 Chronicles 24, Jehoash wanted to renovate the Lord's temple and had to work with others to make this come to fruition. They were only successful because they came together with confidence in their talents and roles—and they listened to God. God calls us to do what is right and to treat each other with respect and care. While ungodly intentions can poison even the most unified of groups, coming together, speaking truth, and seeking God collectively will produce the best results.

If you don't know by now, I truly believe when we come together with God no one can stop us. Remember: "All he has is human strength, but we have the Lord our God, who will help us fight our battles!" (2 Chronicles 32:8)

REFLECTION QUESTIONS

1. **2 Chronicles 20–24:** Why did Jehoash have a hard time working with others to fix God's temple in Chapter 24?

2. **2 Chronicles 25–28:** The prophet warned Amaziah not to worship idols, but he did not listen. When have you regretted not listening to God?

3. **2 Chronicles 29–32:** Why do you think Abijah, the mother of Hezekiah, is mentioned?

4. **2 Chronicles 33–36:** What factors lead to the eventual destruction of Jerusalem?

5. **Psalms 68–72:** Psalm 69:3 reads, "My eyes are exhausted with waiting for my God." Do you think God would view this differently if "my" was changed to "our"?

6. **Psalms 73–78:** Psalm 73:13 says, "Meanwhile, I've kept my heart pure for no good reason." Have you ever felt despair like this? What helped you press on?

POINTS TO PONDER

1. What are the main issues you have working with other people?
2. We don't work together just for a moment; we work with others for life. Who are the people you have worked with multiple times and why?
3. Why were the people in 2 Chronicles 32 successful working together? What did you learn from this story?

VERSE OF THE WEEK

Psalm 73:25–26 reads: "Do I have anyone else in heaven? There's nothing on Earth I desire except you. My body and my heart fail, but God is my heart's rock and my share forever." Reflect on what these words mean to you and how you can walk together with God.

GUIDED PRAYER

Gracious God, thank you for creating me and others. Thank you for bringing us together to make this world a better place. We thank you and honor you. Amen.

WEEK 27

CALLED FOR SUCH A TIME AS THIS

READINGS

Reading 1: Esther 1–3

Reading 2: Esther 4–6

Reading 3: Esther 7–10

Reading 4: Psalms 79–84

Reading 5: Psalms 85–89

Reading 6: Psalms 90–96

WE NEVER KNOW THE EXACT TIME WE WILL be led to speak up and out for ourselves and others. Before we read about Hadassah (Esther 2:7), commonly known as Esther, we learn about a queen by the name of Vashti. Vashti refused to be paraded around as an object in front of her husband and guests. She was made for that moment. Her courage did not receive praise, but she did empower others, perhaps even Esther.

There are many forces that lead us to believe that what we do when confronted with injustice won't matter, but it does. When we lean on God, greater things are birthed into the world—even if we never see them. Esther experienced the same system as Vashti did, but in a different way. She had to make a choice when the odds seemed to be stacked against her.

We may not be excited about everything God wants us to do, but this doesn't mean we shouldn't do them. When we put one foot in front of the other and walk anyway, in the face of opposition, God can show up. Yes, our realities are complex, but I am here to say God cares about the obstacles we face, and you, beloved, are called for such a time as this.

REFLECTION QUESTIONS

1. **Esther 1–3:** What did you learn from Vashti about being called for such a time as this?

2. **Esther 4–6:** Have you ever underestimated yourself as Esther did?

3. **Esther 7–10:** Were there times when you wanted to speak up but didn't know what to say? How can you prepare for future moments like this?

4. **Psalms 79–84:** Meditate for a moment on Psalm 79:4. Have you ever felt like this? What helped you overcome it?

5. **Psalms 85–89:** How would you give hope to someone feeling similar to the author of the psalms in this section?

6. **Psalms 90–96:** What does Psalm 90 tell you about how you can approach life?

POINTS TO PONDER

1. We often see situations like Vashti's in present-day life. Can you think of any present-day examples?
2. How have you dealt with criticism and pressure when making a decision?
3. Bring to mind a time when you met the moment. What did it feel like? What did you learn?

ACTIVITY

Think of a woman you admire who has stood up against injustice. It can be someone you know personally or who you admire from a distance. Write down the characteristics they possess that you look up to. Reflect on how you can exhibit these characteristics in your everyday life.

GUIDED PRAYER

Restore us, God; give us what we need to see the moment and the courage to seize it. Amen.

WEEK 28

MAINTAIN

READINGS

Reading 1: Job 1–3

Reading 2: Job 4–7

Reading 3: Job 8–11

Reading 4: Job 12–14

Reading 5: Job 15–17

Reading 6: Job 18–21

IT'S HARD TO MAINTAIN YOUR BALANCE in life when your world seems to be falling apart all around you. When we experience blind judgment from those who can't understand our experiences and begin to lose the people and things we love, we can become hopeless and even begin to lose our minds. Our situations can look somewhat like Job's predicament.

In order to maintain your grip under certain conditions, you must have something you believe in. In this week's readings, Job's situation is heartbreaking, God is on trial, and there are no answers to why Job faces tribulations. Let this week encourage you to search for your way and hold on to it. You never know when you may need it.

REFLECTION QUESTIONS

1. **Job 4–7:** What reasons does Eliphaz give for Job's suffering?

2. **Job 8–11:** What would you have done differently than Bildad in responding to Job's pain?

---

3. **Job 15–17:** Do you think Job is justified in how he responded in this week's readings? Why or why not?

POINTS TO PONDER

1. Job's wife is often seen as evil. If in court, how would you defend her honesty? (Job 2:9)
2. Have you ever felt like you had nothing to live for? What helped you not give up? (Job 6:11)
3. Saying "I won't complain" is nice, but sometimes we need a moment to express our true feelings. Are there healthy ways to express how you feel and keep your integrity? (Job 6:5)

ACTIVITY

What question have you always wanted to ask God but felt it was inappropriate to do so? Try to make connections with the readings for the week. Remember, we serve a God who can handle our questions.

GUIDED PRAYER

Powerful God, I pray for your protection. I believe and trust you, in the power of God. Amen.

WEEK 29

YOU HAVE TO KNOW

READINGS

Reading 1: Job 22–24

Reading 2: Job 25–28

Reading 3: Job 29–31

Reading 4: Job 32–35

Reading 5: Job 36–39

Reading 6: Job 40–42

LAST WEEK WE BEGAN READING ABOUT THE LIFE OF JOB. During his period of suffering, he experiences silence from God. Even so, he stops short of accusing God of injustice.

Job debates his circumstances with friends, who believe that he must have done something evil to deserve his plight. After they each offer their perspectives about God and Job's current situation, God finally speaks in Job 38. God comes to Job in a whirlwind, proving God speaks and works in ways we can't truly understand. Sometimes, the only way to endure through difficult times is to hold fast to that knowledge.

While your faith will be tested at various points throughout life, what you should know is that there is absolutely nothing you need to or can do to get God to love you more. God loves you and cares about your suffering. What we go through is not an indication of how great God is. Just as God has protected and cared for those before us, God still cares about you, and you just have to know that.

REFLECTION QUESTIONS

1. **Job 22–24:** How does Job respond to Eliphaz?

2. **Job 25–28:** Do you think Job's response and predicament might be different if he were a woman?

3. **Job 29–31:** Which one of Job's friends can you relate to the most?

4. **Job 32–35:** How does the viewpoint of Elihu differ from that of Job?

5. **Job 36–39:** What do these chapters tell you about God?

6. **Job 40–42:** What is the significance of God answering Job in a whirlwind?

POINTS TO PONDER

1. In Job 29, Job begins to compare his former blessings to his current reality. What are your thoughts about the change in Job's tone and reflection on his past?
2. Job didn't back down; we sometimes need to have this posture when dealing with people. When do you stand your ground?
3. In Job 38, God attempts to reorient Job by reintroducing God's self. Have you had a similar experience?

ACTION OF THE WEEK

What do you know without a shadow of doubt about God? In the week ahead, recite the thing you are sure of each morning before you start the day.

GUIDED PRAYER

The God who loves and rescues me from suffering, you are worthy of my praise. Continue to speak and guide me as I experience the ups and downs of life. Amen.

WEEK 30

HIS DESTINY, HER PURPOSE

READINGS

Reading 1: John 1–4

Reading 2: John 5–8

Reading 3: John 9–11

Reading 4: John 12–15

Reading 5: John 16–18

Reading 6: John 19–21

JESUS HAD TO DEAL WITH A LOT WHILE ON EARTH. His actions and bold speech were the opposite of how most members of his society behaved. He was criticized, challenged, and mocked. Maybe you can relate to this. I am sure you've been talked about, left out, and ignored before. It's important to remember none of these things take away your purpose. Your purpose can sometimes bump up against everything you've been told about yourself. But there is something very spiritual about your purpose, made specifically for you, sent from heaven.

The readings this week begin with the acknowledgment of Jesus's divinity: "In the beginning the Word already existed. The Word was with God, and the Word was God. He existed in the beginning with God. God created everything through him, and nothing was created except through him" (John 1:1–3 NLT). If we had to write scripture about our purpose, perhaps it would read, "In the very beginning purpose existed in her. God created her, so therefore her purpose is powerful."

Just as Jesus was rejected and questioned, you may find that others don't see your purpose. What people believe does not change the spirit that empowers you, and it does not change your purpose. Your purpose is a beautiful power.

REFLECTION QUESTIONS

1. **John 1–4:** The Samaritan woman's response in John 4:9 reflects how she is usually treated by society. Did you ever refuse encouragement or affirmation because of past experiences?

2. **John 5–8:** What lesson did you receive from the story of the woman caught in adultery?

3. **John 9–11:** What do you learn about the faith of Mary and her sister Martha in John 11?

4. **John 12–15:** Thinking of the words in John 12:43, have you ever sought praise rather than your greater purpose?

5. **John 16–18:** What stood out to you in these chapters that's different from the other authors' telling of this story?

6. **John 19–21:** Do you think Pilate could have made a different decision? What do his actions tell you about human behavior?

______

______

POINTS TO PONDER

1. Our purpose includes more than just standing there. We must have faith, walk, see, and go forth. Why is it hard to see and go forth? (John 19:25)
2. Do you believe living a purposeful life allows you to live on after you're gone from Earth?
3. It's written in John 9:4: "We must quickly carry out the tasks assigned us by the one who sent us" (NLT). What does this scripture mean to you in relation to your purpose?

ACTIVITY

It's hard to truly believe our purpose if we don't articulate it. To help clarify your purpose, write down your answers to the following questions on a piece of paper. Don't worry about having the "perfect" answers—just be true to who you are.

1. What do you love to do?
2. What are your gifts, passions, and talents?
3. What do you dream about doing?

GUIDED PRAYER

God, when the world can't see my purpose, help me believe in myself. Thank you that I am here and able to honor my purpose. Amen.

WEEK 31

DUE SEASON

READINGS

Reading 1: Ecclesiastes 1–4

Reading 2: Ecclesiastes 5–8

Reading 3: Ecclesiastes 9–12

Reading 4: Psalms 97–100

Reading 5: Psalms 101–103

Reading 6: Psalms 104–106

THE BOOK OF ECCLESIASTES, also known as Qoheleth, addresses the hard questions of life. Many describe this book as dark and despairing, but if we're honest, life can sometimes feel this way. There are times when flowery language and perfect paintings just won't do. We have to ask the hard questions in order to move on in a liberating way. *Why am I doing this if our time on Earth is finite? What is the meaning of life?* I don't know about you, but I've been there. There were moments when I simply needed a reality check.

There were times when I thought "Now I've made it" and that my accomplishments would make me feel good for the rest of my life, but they didn't. When we think we have it all figured out, we may need to take a moment to look around and realize we don't know as much as we thought we did. During these moments, God was asking me to rethink how I view God and life, and in the appropriate hour, things began to make sense.

We all have questions about life's true meaning. God is the only one who can provide us with these answers . . . in our due seasons. There are many confusing joys and sorrows. God can handle our questions, and God also wants us to enjoy the gift of life. Keep searching and never forget that all can be revealed in due season.

REFLECTION QUESTIONS

1. **Ecclesiastes 1–4:** What can you learn in Ecclesiastes about trusting in God's timetable?

2. **Ecclesiastes 5–8:** What is a verse you relate to in these chapters and why?

3. **Ecclesiastes 9–12:** Ecclesiastes 11:6 says, "Plant your seed in the morning and keep busy all afternoon, for you don't know if profit will come from one activity or another." What does this mean to you?

4. **Psalms 97–100:** What affirmation do you find encouraging in these psalms and why?

5. **Psalms 101–103:** Which verse from Psalm 103 would you say to someone who felt like there was no meaning to life?

6. **Psalms 104–106:** Reflect on Psalm 106:4. What salvation do you hope for when you reach your due season?

POINTS TO PONDER

1. "Too much activity gives you restless dreams; too many words make you a fool" (Ecclesiastes 5:3 NLT). What do you do when you are waiting for an answer from God?
2. Working 15 hours a day every day will not get you answers from God any faster than ordained. There is a time to laugh, be free, enjoy life, and rest. How do you find time for balance? (Ecclesiastes 12:12)
3. This week's readings offer reminders of how to center one's mind when life loses its meaning. When has life felt empty, and what has helped you not feel this way?

VERSE OF THE WEEK

Psalm 1:3 reads, "They are like a tree replanted by streams of water, which bears fruit at just the right time and whose leaves don't fade. Whatever they do succeeds." What does this verse mean to you in relation to the seasons of your life?

GUIDED PRAYER

The most powerful One, when I can't see or trace you, remind me of your everlasting presence. Let your presence cover all my insecurities. In your love I pray. Amen.

WEEK 32

OH, WHAT LOVE!

READINGS

Reading 1: Song of Songs 1–4

Reading 2: Song of Songs 5–8

Reading 3: Psalms 107–110

Reading 4: Psalms 111–116

Reading 5: Psalms 117–119

Reading 6: Psalms 120–128

MANY HAVE IDENTIFIED SONG OF SONGS as the last of the wisdom books. These books (Proverbs, Job, Ecclesiastes, Psalms, and Song of Songs) are known as collected wisdom to help people make moral decisions. Song of Songs offers a different tone from previous readings. This book allows us to sit with love in its various forms and expressions. Love is truly special. Love can hurt and heal. Love can free us and lift our spirits. Love is God and God cares about our total being, including our most intimate feelings and desires.

God is never mentioned in the book, but there is an overwhelming idea that love from God and others should feel light and balanced—a love that gives you permission not to be perfect, just to be you. We look at life differently when we have loved and are loved. Oh, what a love!

REFLECTION QUESTIONS

1. **Song of Songs 1–4:** What advice can you pull from these chapters about loving yourself?

2. **Song of Songs 5–8:** The poetry here describes a romantic kind of relationship. How does your romantic life intersect with your spiritual pursuits?

---

3. **Psalms 107–110:** Which verse in these chapters sums up God's love to you?

POINTS TO PONDER

1. Reflect on this verse: "My brothers were angry with me; they forced me to care for their vineyards, so I couldn't care for myself—my own vineyard" (Song of Songs 1:6 NLT). Have you neglected yourself for others in this way?
2. How can you love yourself better?
3. Does the love you experience resemble the love you receive from God? Why and why not? Should it?

ACTIVITY

Describe the love you desire, but make it fun! Write down your own recipe of love. Note the key ingredients, why they are important, and what role they play in your life. Identify the ingredients you already possess and the ones you need to find.

GUIDED PRAYER

Oh God, thank you for loving me. Let me be satisfied with choosing what and who loves me. Let me experience love on Earth that centers and frees me so I, too, can love. Amen.

WEEK 33

I'M NOT WORTHY, BUT I'LL GO

READINGS

Reading 1: Isaiah 1–4

Reading 2: Isaiah 5–8

Reading 3: Isaiah 9–12

Reading 4: Isaiah 13–16

Reading 5: Isaiah 17–20

Reading 6: Isaiah 21–24

NO MATTER OUR CIRCUMSTANCES, we all are worthy; we just don't always feel like it. We all do things we shouldn't, and we put ourselves in situations that don't deserve us. While this is true, God already made us worthy.

In this week's readings, the prophet Isaiah gives voice to God's assessment of a nation that had turned a deaf ear to the Lord. The book unveils the full dimensions of God's judgment and salvation. However, Isaiah was not well-liked because he told the truth. He was trying to open the eyes of defeated people who walked away from their worthiness. We, like them, are often in positions where we have to make a choice in the midst of disobedience, heartache, and uncertainty. We are given the opportunity to go toward something new.

We can make a choice to walk in what God already ordained. We can agree to go, to see, to experience our worthiness. Sister, there must be more for us than this. Just as Isaiah answered the call in the midst of ridicule, we, too, have to go toward God—even when people don't treat us right or do their part, we have to go toward something more. To go signifies going in another direction to embrace our worthiness. We are worthy, and we should go meet God.

REFLECTION QUESTIONS

1. **Isaiah 1–4:** What does Isaiah 4 reveal about the nature of God and people?

2. **Isaiah 5–8:** What was it like for Isaiah to be in the Lord's presence in Isaiah 6?

3. **Isaiah 9–12:** Isaiah describes how God can remove the burdens of people. When has God done this for you?

4. **Isaiah 13–16:** In what ways can you relate to the people of Israel in these chapters?

5. **Isaiah 17–20:** How do you think Isaiah would be perceived today?

6. **Isaiah 21–24:** Isaiah wanted to help the people move in a better direction. How do you deal with people who ignore your efforts to help them?

POINTS TO PONDER

1. Have you ever said yes to something you should have said no to?
2. Even when you mess up, God is always waiting with open arms. Is there anything you've repeated that you shouldn't have?
3. Yes, we all do things that make us feel unworthy. Remind yourself why you are worthy. Complete this sentence and say it out loud: "I am worthy because . . ."

ACTION OF THE WEEK

Sometimes it is hard to decipher what God's voice is telling us to go toward. Reflecting on this week's readings, think of one way that God might be calling you to move in a new direction. Think of one small change you can make to start following the calling and put it into action in the coming week.

GUIDED PRAYER

I thank you, God, for ordaining me worthy. I pray that I continue to see and walk in what I deserve. Amen.

WEEK 34

YOUR NEXT IS NOW

READINGS

Reading 1: Isaiah 25–27

Reading 2: Isaiah 28–31

Reading 3: Isaiah 32–35

Reading 4: Isaiah 36–39

Reading 5: Isaiah 40–42

Reading 6: Isaiah 43–46

WHY IS IT HARD TO UNDERSTAND THAT YOUR NEXT IS NOW? That your next steps just very well may be your best ones yet? It honestly can be hard to see our next when our now is weighing us down. We can go about our days and forget to look around, and we miss God. We even miss opportunities right in front of our faces. Like the people in this week's readings, we are being encouraged to see God moving in our lives right now, regardless of what happened in the past or present.

Isaiah is saying, "Clear the Lord's way in the desert! Make a level highway in the wilderness for our God! Every valley will be raised up, and every mountain and hill will be flattened" (40:3–4). There is nothing God can't do.

God speaks through the prophet Isaiah to encourage the people of Judah not to dwell on how they had to struggle in the past to become a nation, but to carve a path forward instead. God wants this for us today, too.

Something better is always available to you, so just reach out and grab it, and remember it's okay to make room for God—to praise God for your now. God is moving in your life. Surely your next will soon be now—and it looks amazing!

REFLECTION QUESTIONS

1. **Isaiah 25–27:** God answered Isaiah's prayers. What prayers has God answered for you lately?

___

___

2. **Isaiah 28–31:** What does the verse Isaiah 30:21 mean to you?

___

___

3. **Isaiah 32–35:** In Isaiah, we read a lot about condemnation and restoration. Why do you think it was hard for this community to listen and do something new?

___

___

4. **Isaiah 36–39:** In Isaiah 36, the chief of staff tried to intimidate and mislead God's people. How have you dealt with this type of behavior in your life?

___

___

5. **Isaiah 40–42:** Isaiah 40:8 is a well-known verse that is recited often. What does it tell us about life on Earth and the enduring Word of God?

___

___

6. **Isaiah 43–46:** What hope do you find in Isaiah 43?

POINTS TO PONDER

1. We sometimes think we have to wait to step into our next, like "I have to wait until I'm 30 to go back to school." Have societal expectations ever led you to not appreciate your now?
2. Isaiah covers a variety of themes, including holiness and hope, as well as salvation through the coming Messiah. What does Isaiah reveal to you about God?
3. "The grass withers and the flowers fade, but the word of our God stands forever" (Isaiah 40:8 NLT). This is commonly referenced in scripture. What does this scripture mean to you when thinking about your next being now?

ACTIVITY

Hezekiah's Poem of Praise can be found in Isaiah 38. Reread this, then come up with a saying of praise claiming your next to be now.

GUIDED PRAYER

God, help me see what you are doing around me. Give me the courage to embrace and walk fearlessly into my next. Amen.

WEEK 35

THINK BIG

READINGS

Reading 1: Isaiah 47–49

Reading 2: Isaiah 50–53

Reading 3: Isaiah 54–57

Reading 4: Isaiah 58–60

Reading 5: Isaiah 61–63

Reading 6: Isaiah 64–66

THIS WEEK, IN ISAIAH 55:8 WE READ, "'My thoughts are nothing like your thoughts,' says the Lord. 'And my ways are far beyond anything you could imagine.'"

Eyes have not seen and ears have not heard of what God has for us. Thinking big changes everything you have learned is and isn't possible. It changes everything the world says you should be. It can even challenge everything you have read about being a woman. When we think big, we shake things up. We disrupt all the small ideas people put on us: "She will be just like her mother"; "There is no way she'll graduate college."

We are not meant to remain in boxes or these defined positions. God wants us to not only think big but believe in what we think, even when factors don't add up and situations don't reflect this. Sister, thinking *big* is claiming your place in this world! Sometimes, we have to change our thoughts to see how big God is.

REFLECTION QUESTIONS

1. **Isaiah 47–49:** People can sometimes limit how we think about and view God (Isaiah 47:13). How has this shown up in your life?

2. **Isaiah 58–60:** "I said, 'Here I am, here I am!' to a nation that did not call on my name" (Isaiah 65:1 NLT). What are you calling God for?

---

3. **Isaiah 61–63:** We can think of verse 61:1 as Isaiah's purpose statement. What is yours?

POINTS TO PONDER

1. Thinking big helps you take limits off God. How have you limited God with your thinking?
2. What is something new that you can try to help you think differently?
3. Do you think people want to think big, or is it more comfortable for us to stay where we are?

VERSE OF THE WEEK

Isaiah 51:7 tells us, "Do not be afraid of people's scorn, nor fear their insults" (NLT). In what practical ways can you embody this scripture?

GUIDED PRAYER

God, thank you for changing my thought to see how big you are. Help me to never limit you and see just how big my life is. Amen.

WEEK 36

PRAYER STILL WORKS

READINGS

Reading 1: Acts 1–3

Reading 2: Acts 4–7

Reading 3: Acts 8–10

Reading 4: Acts 11–14

Reading 5: Acts 15–17

Reading 6: Acts 18–21

IN THE READINGS FOR THIS WEEK, the disciples and other believers of the way were experiencing amazing things through prayer. They were healing people, evoking the Holy Spirit, challenging social lies, and attracting more followers. Prayer definitely shifted the atmosphere. Their connections to God rearranged almost every space they entered; prayer was their protection.

In the same way prayer worked in the scriptures, prayer still works for you. Prayer has a way to calm, push, and liberate us.

Listen: Prayer still works.

Prayer helps us do the work and live out what God has mandated us to do. Prayer is powerful and should never be used to counter the ways of God. Prayer helps God fulfill plans with patience and majesty. Prayer helps us communicate with God in ways we never could with people. Prayer is our time with God. It's a way to connect to power that pushes things back together. When things come together, not only do we benefit, but everyone benefits. Prayer is communication, and without communication, nothing can work. Remember, prayer can help all chains fall off more than once (Acts 16:25).

REFLECTION QUESTIONS

1. **Acts 1–3:** The healing of the crippled man can be a form of prayer in action. What prayer in action have you heard of or experienced lately?

2. **Acts 4–7:** In Acts 4:23, a community of believers prays. Why is it important to pray with and for others?

3. **Acts 8–10:** Saul wreaked havoc on the church. Do you pray for those you're connected to who do what they shouldn't? Why or why not?

4. **Acts 11–14:** Peter was freed from prison by God. How do you think God feels about mass incarceration today?

5. **Acts 15–17:** When prayers are answered, accountability and integrity must follow (Acts 16:37). What does this look like in your life?

6. **Acts 18–21:** God can move in miraculous ways as he did for Paul in Acts 19:11. How has God moved in your life since beginning this reading journey?

POINTS TO PONDER

1. Praise and prayer are two different things. We can sometimes praise the people following God and forget to pray to God. Have you experienced this?
2. When did you begin to believe in prayer?
3. There are people who we know will pray for us. Who is your prayer partner and why?

ACTIVITY

Women are often mentioned in the readings, some by name and others unnamed. Take around five minutes to see what scriptures you can find that include women and reflect on the context of their situations. Bonus points for scriptures that describe women praying and being spiritual leaders.

GUIDED PRAYER

Oh God, who hears my prayers, help me not question your power and fix my heart to believe without a shadow of doubt that prayer still works. Amen.

WEEK 37

YOU WILL MAKE IT

READINGS

Reading 1: Acts 22–25

Reading 2: Acts 26–28

Reading 3: Jeremiah 1–3

Reading 4: Jeremiah 4–6

Reading 5: Jeremiah 7–11

Reading 6: Jeremiah 12–15

SOME EVENTS AND EXPERIENCES ARE AVOIDABLE, some not so much. We never really know how our lives will pan out. In Acts 22, Paul tells of his past life and helps us see this to be true. While no one should make any excuse for the devastation Paul caused, I do wonder how many thought his path would take such a drastic turn.

He went from causing terror to those who believed in Jesus to using the power of Jesus's name to set people free. Sometimes, you will meet unlikely people on your journey who can show you that you will make it. There are always unlikely ways God can reassure us of this.

I don't know what you are going through as you're reading this. And while I am not sure what you've been through, I am sure that God finds ways for us to make it. I'm not saying what you are experiencing isn't hard. All I'm saying is that you can make it. Even if you've been called to a difficult assignment, you will make it, and when you make it, be sure you hold someone's hand to help them do the same.

REFLECTION QUESTIONS

1. **Acts 22–25:** Do you think Paul should have been forgiven by those who were affected by his actions?

2. **Acts 26–28:** In Acts 27:23, an angel reassured Paul he would survive the storm. How has God showed you that you will make it?

3. **Jeremiah 1–3:** What reassurance do you find in Jeremiah 1?

4. **Jeremiah 4–6:** What do truth, justice, and righteousness look like to God in these chapters?

5. **Jeremiah 7–11:** Jeremiah questioned the actions of the people. What challenges are there in going against the grain of society for God?

6. **Jeremiah 12–15:** What were some of the reasons the people in these readings didn't believe they could make it?

POINTS TO PONDER

1. In what ways does God help us through difficult times in our lives?
2. In what ways can we be a channel for God's love and grace to help others who are experiencing troubles in their lives?
3. How would you answer this question in Jeremiah 12:1? "If I took you to court, Lord, you would win. But I still have questions about your justice. Why do guilty persons enjoy success? Why are evildoers so happy?"

ACTION OF THE WEEK

There are days we all feel like giving up. Find a verse from this week's readings that can encourage you during these times. Let it be a motto for you as you encounter any challenges in the week ahead.

GUIDED PRAYER

God, when I feel like giving up, help me see you. Send exactly what I need when I need it. I count my breakthrough done. Amen.

WEEK 38

GOD KEPT ME

READINGS

IN JEREMIAH 20, God continued to speak to Jeremiah, and he was obedient. His obedience did not mean people listened or even respected him. Pashhur, the priest in charge of the Temple, decided to whip, arrest, and place Jeremiah in stocks because of the truth he spoke. Jeremiah was consistent and knew his calling, and yet destruction was all around him. This was no easy life.

These are moments where we look back and wonder, *How did I make it?* I've learned that when I was faced with the most challenging of circumstances, it's truly God who kept me safe. Oftentimes, God gives us command over situations, even when we are confined like Jeremiah. Remember, God can keep you safe.

REFLECTION QUESTIONS

1. **Jeremiah 16–19:** Jeremiah reminded the people how God kept them. What is the earliest memory you have of God keeping you?

2. **Jeremiah 20–22:** Jeremiah disrupted unhealthy and hurtful political and communal practices. How do you think God was working on his behalf?

---

3. **Jeremiah 23–26:** What is the promise of restoration in Jeremiah 23?

POINTS TO PONDER

1. Jeremiah 29:11 is a popular verse of the Bible, but it's often quoted without context. How does knowing the situation of the exiles help you better understand that verse?
2. As women, we sometimes deal with others not listening to us. Think of a time this happened to you. How did you deal with this?
3. When God keeps us, we should see a change in ourselves. How has God's protection changed you?

VERSE OF THE WEEK

Reread Jeremiah 29:11: "I know the plans I have in mind for you, declares the Lord; they are plans for peace, not disaster, to give you a future filled with hope." Meditate on the promises of this verse as you choose to be prayerfully present in your life this week.

GUIDED PRAYER

God, thank you for keeping me. Help me hear you when I feel like giving up. Help me remember your love and always seek you. Amen.

WEEK 39

PURPOSE AND PROCESS

READINGS

Reading 1: Jeremiah 38–41

Reading 2: Jeremiah 42–45

Reading 3: Jeremiah 46–49

Reading 4: Jeremiah 50–52

Reading 5: Lamentations 1–2

Reading 6: Lamentations 3–5

IF YOU THINK ABOUT IT, everything must go through a process of growth. Flowers begin with seeds; butterflies develop in cocoons; and, for us, from infancy to adulthood, life unfolds in many ways. When we are put to the test, the process of change can feel frustrating, even defeating at times. However, a process can be filled with purpose, too. In fact, when we don't go through a process, it's hard to achieve growth or begin to believe there's even beauty in it.

Reflect on the trials of Jeremiah from this week's reading: He was locked up for years for delivering the Word of the Lord, but he didn't let that stop him. In fact, confronted with a dark chapter in his life, he called on the name of the Lord and held his faith.

It isn't always easy to predict what will happen in our lives, especially when we are thrown off course by other people rather than by God. There are some interferences we didn't see coming, and even God may be surprised. When this happens, you will likely need to go through a process of growth.

This begins by turning to God, trusting in God's process, and knowing that the challenges you face can't erase your purpose. We face and experience many overwhelming things, but I believe we serve a God that cares and can take a messy process and create lasting legacies.

REFLECTION QUESTIONS

1. **Jeremiah 38–41:** These chapters show how others are affected by our decisions. How often do you think about others in your everyday actions?

2. **Jeremiah 42–45:** In Jeremiah 42, Johanan and other leaders ask for a message from God but refuse to listen. How is this connected to purpose and process?

3. **Jeremiah 46–49:** In these chapters, many nations received messages from God. What does this say about God and the world?

4. **Jeremiah 50–52:** You could say that the people of Israel's process was interrupted. Do you think this was ordained by God?

5. **Lamentations 1–2:** Scholars have suggested that the author of Lamentations could have been a woman. What do you think about this?

6. **Lamentations 3–5:** Sometimes poems express pain in ways other forms of communication cannot. What verses in these chapters can you relate to and why?

POINTS TO PONDER

1. Are there any additional scriptures from the Bible you know that can help you think about process and purpose?
2. Do you think there is a beginning point and ending point to a process? Or is life itself an unfolding process?
3. If you had to give advice to anyone about a difficult process being purposeful, what would it be?

ACTIVITY

Put yourself in the shoes of someone experiencing the hard times (such as suffering or famine) in Lamentations. Take a few minutes to come up with a short poem or some words that express what they were going through.

GUIDED PRAYER

God, I pray over my process that it always makes room for my purpose. Help me breathe and see you in every way. Amen.

WEEK 40

JUST SPEAK IT

READINGS

Reading 1: Ezekiel 1–3

Reading 2: Ezekiel 4–7

Reading 3: Ezekiel 8–11

Reading 4: Ezekiel 12–15

Reading 5: Ezekiel 16–18

Reading 6: Ezekiel 19–21

THERE ARE TIMES WHEN GOD MUST PREPARE us and give us the words to deal with situations we've never experienced. In Ezekiel 3:9–10, God says to the prophet Ezekiel, "I've made your forehead like a diamond, harder than stone. Don't be afraid of them or shrink away from them, because they are a household of rebels . . . Listen closely, and take to heart every word I say to you."

While the graphic imagery and violent language in this week's readings can be difficult to read at times, there is a valuable message in the story of Ezekiel. He is noted by scholars as a priest and prophet who lived in the time leading up to after the Babylonian invasion of Judah. Ezekiel was deported to Babylon and commanded to convey information from God to people who refused to listen while also dealing with his own issues and pain.

Before Ezekiel could speak, he had to believe—and we must, too. We can do so knowing that God has made our hearts and minds strong like diamonds. When we listen to what God tells us, we can believe that our words have meaning in order to speak our truth. So, in the midst of doubters and difficulties, just speak it.

REFLECTION QUESTIONS

1. **Ezekiel 1–3:** What greater message do you see in God instructing Ezekiel to eat the scroll?

2. **Ezekiel 4–7:** Ezekiel was placed in what many would categorize as an uncomfortable position. How do you handle speaking out in uncomfortable moments?

3. **Ezekiel 8–11:** Why does God's glory leave the temple?

4. **Ezekiel 12–15:** Which of Ezekiel's stories stands out to you the most and why?

5. **Ezekiel 16–18:** Ezekiel 18 reveals the importance of leading people in a healthy way. Are there things people have told you that led you down dark paths? How did you see the light?

6. **Ezekiel 19–21:** In Ezekiel 20, the people come to Ezekiel to hear from God, yet God questions their actions. What does this mean?

POINTS TO PONDER

1. What similarities and differences do you see between the prophets Jeremiah and Ezekiel?
2. How can living in God's strength and truth help us through ups and downs? How can it empower us to help others?
3. Think of a personal goal based on this week's lesson.

ACTION OF THE WEEK

This week, challenge yourself to pray out loud. This can help you articulate your inner feelings and clarify what you wish to communicate with God. Speak your truth and take it to God!

GUIDED PRAYER

Gracious and powerful God, help me speak out loud the things I need from you. Help me speak truth in the midst of challenges. Amen.

WEEK 41

LESSON LEARNED

READINGS

Reading 1: Ezekiel 22–24

Reading 2: Ezekiel 25–28

Reading 3: Ezekiel 29–32

Reading 4: Ezekiel 33–36

Reading 5: Ezekiel 37–39

Reading 6: Ezekiel 40–42

MY GRANDFATHER PASSED AWAY A MONTH AFTER I graduated college. I remember exactly what I said during the remarks at his funeral: "I've sat in the classroom with some of the most brilliant professors, and my grandfather who never graduated high school was my best teacher." It's been 10 years since then, and this statement still holds true.

My grandfather guided me with not just his words, but also his actions. From a talk on his deck to a late-night phone call, he was always teaching me. He showed me that lessons come in many forms, and if we're not paying attention, we can miss them. In this week's readings, we learn more about the prophet Ezekiel and his role as a watchman over the people of Israel when they were captive in Babylon. In Ezekiel 33:5, we are reminded of the need to stay alert to the messages in our lives and their greater meaning: "They heard the sound of the trumpet but didn't heed the warning, so their blood is on them. If they had paid attention to the warning, they would have saved their lives."

We can't learn or grow without lessons. You never know when you will need them or when you will use the information. To have it is the gift. Remember, lessons can come at any time, so sit up and get your pencil, because class is in session.

REFLECTION QUESTIONS

1. **Ezekiel 22–24:** Can you relate to the people of Israel and their "disobedience"?

2. **Ezekiel 25–28:** What lessons are there in the prophetic message of Ezekiel?

3. **Ezekiel 29–32:** How do the Egyptians use and manipulate the people of Judah?

4. **Ezekiel 33–36:** Ezekiel 33 centers on community and the importance of actions. How do your words match your actions?

5. **Ezekiel 37–39:** When God asked Ezekiel to prophesy over dry bones, Ezekiel was putting his learning into action. How have you put your lessons into action?

6. **Ezekiel 40–42:** Ezekiel uses a lot of symbolic language. How can symbolism like this help us learn lessons?

POINTS TO PONDER

1. Lessons have different meanings as we gain life experience. What lessons have changed in their meaning for you?
2. What is the purpose of a lesson?
3. What is a common lesson that the people of Israel learned? Find scripture from this week's readings that describes the lesson.

ACTIVITY

Ezekiel is known as one of the most interesting and troubled prophets in the Bible. Identify and write down five interesting facts about Ezekiel. Reflect on the things that inspire you about his story.

GUIDED PRAYER

Dear God, who loves and cares for me, thank you for the lessons I've learned and help me heed your directions and instruction. Amen.

WEEK 42

I KNOW WHO I AM

READINGS

Reading 1: Ezekiel 43–45

Reading 2: Ezekiel 46–48

Reading 3: Daniel 1–4

Reading 4: Daniel 5–8

Reading 5: Daniel 9–12

Reading 6: Psalms 129–135

WHEN YOU KNOW WHO YOU ARE, no one can shake your sense of identity. You are able to walk boldly in your uniqueness. Unfortunately, when you're confident in who you are, often people will test you, just like they tested Daniel in this week's readings.

In Daniel 6:3, we learn that he was promoted and given additional responsibilities: "Because of his extraordinary spirit, Daniel soon surpassed the other officers and the chief administrators—so much so that the king had plans to set him over the entire kingdom."

His colleagues were jealous and tried to use Daniel's beliefs against him. So, these officers and chief administrators ganged together and enticed the king to enforce a law. This law penalized anyone who prayed to any god or human other than the king.

This happens to us. We are faced with tests and can be thrown into the pit with lions. Daniel was confident in who he was and what he believed. His actions were directly connected to his being. When you know who you are, what you hear will not misdirect you.

Sister, when they try to tell you who you are, when they try to offer you something that does not align with your character, remember you are greatly treasured by God and tell them, "I know who I am."

REFLECTION QUESTIONS

1. **Ezekiel 43–45:** Why do you think the details God gave Ezekiel in reference to the altar were important?

2. **Ezekiel 46–48:** Ezekiel offers a vision of what the nation of Israel can be. How does God show you who you are?

3. **Daniel 1–4:** What did you learn from Shadrach, Meshach, and Abednego about being confident in who you are?

4. **Daniel 5–8:** How do the officers and chief administrators attempt to conspire against Daniel?

5. **Daniel 9–12:** In Daniel 9, the angel Gabriel reassures Daniel. How have you been reassured lately?

6. **Psalms 129–135:** Knowing yourself allows you to see the world with greater clarity. What is a verse in this section that helps you see God more clearly and why?

POINTS TO PONDER

1. In Daniel 2:49, Daniel urges the king to also appoint Shadrach, Meshach, and Abednego. Those who know us can sometimes help us see ourselves. Can you relate?
2. Recall a time when others led you astray from who you are. What did you learn from this experience?
3. What lessons from this week's readings can help us stay true to ourselves?

VERSE OF THE WEEK

Daniel 11:32 tells us, "The people who acknowledge their God will stand strong and will act." Reflect on how you can lean on God to remember who you are this week. How do you think this will positively influence the decisions you make?

GUIDED PRAYER

Help me see who I am when people are working against me. Remind me, God, and give me what I need as I move closer to you. Amen.

WEEK 43

GOD'S MERCY ENDURES

READINGS

Reading 1: Psalms 136–142

Reading 2: Psalms 143–150

Reading 3: Romans 1–4

Reading 4: Romans 5–8

Reading 5: Romans 9–12

Reading 6: Romans 13–16

IT CAN BE HARD TO BELIEVE THAT GOD'S MERCY endures when you turn on the news. At any given time, we find suffering and grief in the world. *Where is God's mercy?* you quietly wonder. This is a question many in our readings asked and a question many of us (including myself) ask today.

It is during these times that I turn to the refuge of prayer, even when it feels hard to do. I pray when pain seems to infiltrate every news station and newspaper. These moments of prayer give birth to remembrance of God's eternal mercy. Of course, God is not responsible for the suffering of the world, but his grace is always there when we have suffered.

Psalm 136 is a special psalm, with each one of its 26 verses repeating the sentence, "His mercy endures forever" (EHV). We may not always experience great weeks or even months, but this psalm reminds us to hold tight to God's mercy.

When they doubt you, remember, God's mercy endures. When dealing with the challenges of family and friend relationships, remember, God's mercy endures. When faced with trials and tribulations, remember, God's mercy endures. When we can do this, we are able to truly live, rather than merely tolerate our situations. We are able to breathe in peace without panic. We are able to make it to see another day, because God's mercy endures.

REFLECTION QUESTIONS

1. **Psalms 136–142:** Psalm 135 shows praise for God's mercy. How do you see God's mercy in your life?

2. **Psalms 143–150:** Psalm 149 calls for praise to be in the mouths of God's people. How do you express your praise for God?

3. **Romans 1–4:** Romans 2:11 says, "God does not have favorites." What does this mean?

4. **Romans 5–8:** How would you explain Romans 5:1–5 in your own words?

5. **Romans 9–12:** Romans 11:29 tells us that "God's gifts and calling can't be taken back." What gifts has God given you?

6. **Romans 13–16:** What type of mercy does God express for the women of Romans 16?

____

____

POINTS TO PONDER

1. Do you think there are limits to God's mercy? There are no right or wrong answers. Refer to the scripture of Psalms to explain your answer.
2. How can we model God's mercy in our interactions with others?
3. What verse resonated with you the most this week and why?

ACTIVITY

God's mercy extends not just to certain groups of people but to all, including women. Take a look at Romans 16 and write down all the women's names mentioned. Which of the women do you find most interesting or inspiring and why?

GUIDED PRAYER

Merciful God, I come to you acknowledging that the world is not perfect, and you, God, can help me see your love in the midst of it all. You are my refuge in whom I trust. Amen.

WEEK 44

GOD IS MAKING IT UP TO YOU

READINGS

Reading 1: Hosea 1–5

Reading 2: Hosea 6–10

Reading 3: Hosea 11–14

Reading 4: Joel 1–3

Reading 5: Amos 1–5

Reading 6: Amos 6–9

UNUSUALLY FOR THE MINOR PROPHETS, there is little to no background information provided about Joel, and yet the message of the book of Joel is clear. Throughout the book, we are warned to turn back to God because there is much for us: "Return to the Lord your God, for he is merciful and compassionate, slow to get angry and filled with unfailing love. God is eager to relent and not punish" (Joel 2:13 NLT).

There are some things we must take back and other things only God can restore. To believe this, we have to admit that life is not easy and we don't always do what's right. We deserve and should want more for our lives. God knows this, but do you? You may feel that you missed or messed up opportunities. You may have lost material things or experienced great griefs, like the loss of a loved one. God can sense voids and makes up for what has been taken from us. God makes up for things we never grabbed or blessings we misused.

God doesn't have to, but God does it anyway. God's love extends to mountains and valleys. God can always replace anything lost and make all things right and whole again.

God is making it up to you!

REFLECTION QUESTIONS

1. **Hosea 1–5:** God commands Gomer to give her children names that reflect anger toward the people of Israel. How do you feel about this?

2. **Hosea 6–10:** What imagery stands out to you about how the people of Israel had gotten away from God's heart?

3. **Hosea 11–14:** What reassurance does God provide to the people of Israel?

4. **Joel 1–3:** In Joel 1, there is a time to lament and mourn. How does this show up in your life?

5. **Amos 1–5:** Why did Amos have a word for people in various places?

6. **Amos 6–9:** What is God's anger directed toward in these chapters?

POINTS TO PONDER

1. What scripture in Joel was most meaningful in relation to your own life?
2. God doesn't bring people back physically. How do you think God helps us through this?
3. Even if we walk away from God, God walks toward us. How have you experienced this?

ACTION OF THE WEEK

When is the last time you decluttered? Scan your space and consider what you can reorganize. You might declutter your purse, closet, desk, or a room in your home. Take inventory. Is there something there you thought you had lost or that you realized you need? Remember, when we do the work, we give space for God to move.

GUIDED PRAYER

I am grateful to you, God, that you can replace, restore, and redirect me. Thank you for loving me so that I can experience and see things I never thought I would again. I am grateful. Amen.

WEEK 45

WAITING ON GOD

READINGS

Reading 1: Obadiah 1

Reading 2: Jonah 1–4

Reading 3: Micah 1–4

Reading 4: Micah 5–7

Reading 5: Nahum 1–3

Reading 6: Habakkuk 1–3

WHAT HAPPENS WHEN YOU WAIT ON God and what you hear is not what you expected? The prophet Jonah had some experience with this. In Jonah 4, we find him distraught that God chose to spare the people of Nineveh, saying, "Didn't I say before I left home that you would do this, Lord? That is why I ran away to Tarshish!" (NLT) Jonah wanted the people of Nineveh to be punished, believing them to be enemies of Israel and Judah, but didn't look in the mirror. He felt like the outcome of actually listening to God wasn't worth it. He was furious, and God was patient with him. Jonah, in his anger, stormed off and waited. It was in the waiting that God offered protection, even if it was only for a period of time.

Woman of God, there is much for us to learn while we wait. When we wait, we may not like what we learn about ourselves. God can handle our anger, but can we handle the lesson? God told Jonah that all are worthy of forgiveness and another chance. Just try it and see.

REFLECTION QUESTIONS

1. **Obadiah 1:** The Edomites took pleasure in the suffering of God's people. Have you ever mistreated others or been mistreated while waiting on God? What did you learn?

2. **Jonah 1–4:** Like Jonah, did you ever try to run from God? What was the outcome?

3. **Micah 1–4:** The prophets spoke out loud, and people didn't listen. What does this tell us about missing signs that are right before our eyes?

4. **Micah 5–7:** What lessons can you pull from these chapters about waiting on God?

5. **Nahum 1–3:** In a sentence, summarize the intended message of the book of Nahum.

6. **Habakkuk 1–3:** In Habakkuk 1:1–3, the prophet asks questions of God, which are then answered. What questions do you have for God in your waiting?

POINTS TO PONDER

1. Many times, people struggle to find the patience to wait on God. What are the consequences of this?
2. Micah 6:8 says, "He has told you, human one, what is good and what the Lord requires from you: to do justice, embrace faithful love, and walk humbly with your God." How can we apply this scripture to our times of waiting?
3. Identify three key lessons from Jonah in the week's readings that resonate with you.

ACTION OF THE WEEK

Spend a minute or two reflecting on the benefits of waiting on God—whether it's an example from your own life, one you have observed, or something hypothetical. Think of how you can carry this lesson forward and put it into action in the week ahead.

GUIDED PRAYER

God, protect me as I wait on you. Give me the courage to wait and the will to see the lesson in the wait. Amen.

WEEK 46

THANK GOD FOR GRACE

READINGS

Reading 1: 1 Corinthians 1–4

Reading 2: 1 Corinthians 5–8

Reading 3: 1 Corinthians 9–12

Reading 4: 1 Corinthians 13–16

Reading 5: 2 Corinthians 1–6

Reading 6: 2 Corinthians 7–13

REGARDLESS OF WHAT WE BELIEVE, how many times we read the Bible, or how much scripture we memorize, we all need and deserve grace. God wants us to be successful and to enjoy the fullness of life. We can't do this without grace, and God is grace. For those of us who have experienced life, we also know it doesn't always feel like we are on the receiving end of grace, as though grace can be inappropriately distributed.

In 2 Corinthians 1:12, Paul says, "This is why we are confident, and our conscience confirms this. We didn't act with human wisdom but we relied on the grace of God." Paul forgot to mention that not acting on human wisdom has different consequences based on who you are.

For some of us, there are factors beyond our control, such as discrimination we may face, that impede our ability to believe we receive God's grace. As women, we may encounter challenges that make it feel like grace is beyond reach at times. Nothing is absolutely guaranteed for anyone, and there is nothing we can do on our own, yet faith can take us a long way and help us see grace. Just like we say our grace before we eat, thank God that we have an opportunity to see a new world. So, rest knowing there is more and you have already received grace from God to get there.

REFLECTION QUESTIONS

1. **1 Corinthians 1–4:** Why do you think Paul wrote this letter to the church of Corinth?

2. **1 Corinthians 5–8:** What verse in these chapters stands out to you the most and why?

3. **1 Corinthians 9–12:** How does 1 Corinthians 10:23 show us how to live in God's grace?

4. **1 Corinthians 13–16:** In 1 Corinthians 13, faith, hope, and love are highlighted as important. How have you exercised these actions this week?

5. **2 Corinthians 1–6:** Paul states, "We didn't act with human wisdom but we relied on the grace of God" (2 Corinthians 1:12). What does this mean to you?

6. **2 Corinthians 7–13:** In 2 Corinthians 7:5 Paul mentions conflicts on every side. How can you better rely on God's grace during moments of conflict in your life?

____

____

POINTS TO PONDER

1. 2 Corinthians 4:8–9 tells us, "We are experiencing all kinds of trouble, but we aren't crushed. We are confused, but we aren't depressed. We are harassed, but we aren't abandoned. We are knocked down, but we aren't knocked out." What insights can be gleaned from this verse?
2. Paul's ideas of women during this time bump up against the idea of God's grace. What areas of tension do you see in the readings?
3. What additional scriptures provide encouragement to those who cannot see or believe in God's grace?

ACTIVITY

Paul wrote two letters to the church of Corinth, and each carries a somewhat different tone. Take five minutes to find out what you can about who he was writing these letters to and reflect on any connections you see in current society.

GUIDED PRAYER

Thank you, God, for your grace. Thank you that there is always room to do more and live more fully in your grace. Amen.

WEEK 47

EXPECT IT, SEE IT, ACHIEVE IT

READINGS

Reading 1: Zephaniah 1–3

Reading 2: Haggai 1–2

Reading 3: Zechariah 1–5

Reading 4: Zechariah 6–10

Reading 5: Zechariah 11–14

Reading 6: Malachi 1–4

WE SHOULD HAVE GREAT EXPECTATIONS. When there is no expectation, it's hard to see or achieve anything. To expect has its pros and cons. We can expect the impossible and be left disappointed. It happened to me. While looking for a job, after being turned down several times, I would often say, "I'm waiting to hear back, but I'm not expecting anything. I'm going with the flow." The word "No" led me to believe I couldn't expect something more in the midst of disappointment. I had to change the way I thought about expectations. Now, I expect what God has for me. I anticipate it will be more. So I refuse to stunt my growth and I continue to walk toward my goals, knowing achievement will come.

In Zechariah 8:4–5, God promises to restore the faithful to Jerusalem: "Old men and old women will again dwell in the plazas of Jerusalem. Each of them will have a staff in their hand because of their great age. The city will be full of boys and girls playing in its plazas." Before the people could get there, they first had to believe this would happen.

We can bring this lesson into our own lives. No matter what we are going through, we must first envision a better tomorrow before it can come to pass. When we expect it, we can see it and we can achieve it.

REFLECTION QUESTIONS

1. **Zephaniah 1–3:** Zephaniah tells of God's wrath and hope. How do you feel this book differs from the other prophetic books?

2. **Haggai 1–2:** The people in the book of Haggai could not truly believe in what God had for them. Why was that? Do you expect things from God in the same way you do from people? What is the difference?

3. **Zechariah 1–5:** God gave the prophets vision. What has God shown you?

4. **Zechariah 6–10:** What contrasts can you observe in the parallel pictures given in Zechariah 7 and 8?

5. **Zechariah 11–14:** In Zechariah 11:15–17, we read, "I will give this nation a shepherd who will not care for those who are dying, nor look after the young" (NLT). How has leadership affected how you see and expect things for your future?

6. **Malachi 1–4:** What do you learn from the book of Malachi about reevaluating the way you think and behave to get to new places?

____

____

POINTS TO PONDER

1. How do you set expectations?
2. What are the challenges of setting expectations? What should people be mindful of?
3. The people of Judah compared their present to their past. Have you done this? If so, how did this affect how you viewed expectations?

ACTIVITY

What are your expectations for your future? On a piece of paper, write down five goals you have for the next month and five more you have for the next year. Place this piece of paper near a mirror or a location where you can see it. Having it visible will encourage you to take small steps towards achieving your goals each week.

GUIDED PRAYER

God, help me see when I feel like giving up. Help me expect more of myself and for my life. You've done it before and can do it again. Amen.

WEEK 48

GETTING BACK TO WHERE I WAS

READINGS

Reading 1: Ezra 1–5

Reading 2: Ezra 6–10

Reading 3: Nehemiah 1–3

Reading 4: Nehemiah 4–7

Reading 5: Nehemiah 8–10

Reading 6: Nehemiah 11–13

WHEN WE STRAY AWAY FROM GOD, away from who we are, it can be hard to get back to where we were. It takes work, determination, and commitment. It takes a clear mind and travel companions who are purehearted people with our well-being in mind.

The book of Ezra provides an account of the return of God's people from Babylon to Jerusalem, of their struggle to survive, and of their yearning to rebuild what had been destroyed. In Ezra 1, those who were exiled prepared to return from captivity after a long time away from their place of comfort and belonging.

To get back home to a place of happiness is no easy task. It takes an undoing; it takes thinking about our lives and how we can engage with the world differently. It takes redefining our womanhood, friendships, and relationships. Getting back to God is a journey, and no journey is ever easy.

Be reminded: If God got us there before, God can do it again. You can always find your way, and when people ask you why you are doing what you are doing, simply respond, "I'm getting back to where I was. I'm getting back to the place that gives me peace and understanding." When you reach this place, trust me, you will know, and God is waiting on you!

REFLECTION QUESTIONS

1. **Ezra 1–5:** The exiled people of Ezra 2 face many attacks on their way back. What trials have you experienced trying to get back to where you were?

2. **Ezra 6–10:** What do you admire about how those who return from captivity complete the temple?

3. **Nehemiah 1–3:** Nehemiah gave a confessional prayer in Nehemiah 1. What would your prayer to God sound like in the hopes of getting to a better place in your life?

4. **Nehemiah 4–7:** In Nehemiah 4, the people face opposition. What opposition have you faced in the process of getting back to where you were?

5. **Nehemiah 8–10:** Why do you think it was important for the Israelites to recount their history and remember who they were in Nehemiah 9?

6. **Nehemiah 11–13:** People come from various places to celebrate the dedication of Jerusalem's wall in Nehemiah 12. How do you share your spiritual joys with others?

POINTS TO PONDER

1. There are often stigmas around going back to something. An example is being over the age of 30 and moving back in with your parents. What stigmas have you heard of or experienced?
2. In Nehemiah 4, armed guards protected the builders as they continued their task. It's important to protect our growth. What are healthy ways to do this?
3. What are some things you will never again jeopardize about yourself?

ACTIVITY

Reflecting on this week's readings, write down one practical way someone can get back to a more peaceful place after experiencing difficult moments in their life. How can you apply this to your own life?

GUIDED PRAYER

Gracious Redeemer, help me get back to where I was. Help me to feel your love and presence in my life. Amen.

WEEK 49

GO FOR IT!

READINGS

Reading 1: Galatians 1–6

Reading 2: Ephesians 1–6

Reading 3: Philippians 1–4

Reading 4: Colossians 1–4

Reading 5: 1 Thessalonians 1–5

Reading 6: 2 Thessalonians 1–3

IT'S ALWAYS INSPIRING TO SEE PEOPLE GO after their dreams. I especially love it when people go after something that they once feared. It brings me joy to know that doing so can lead to so many possibilities and opportunities. You never know what can happen unless you go for it.

I also know there are many things that can cause us to pause or stop: Obstacles can make our anxiety run high, and others' opinions can make us backtrack and wonder if we should move forward. The what-ifs can take over our minds, and what should have been a regathering process becomes a complete stop.

In Ephesians 5:15–16, Paul says, "So be careful to live your life wisely, not foolishly. Take advantage of every opportunity because these are evil times." Here, Paul encouraged the Christians in the ancient city of Ephesus to make the most of their time, despite the persecution and opposition they may have faced.

What opportunities have you let go of because of fear? What didn't you go for that you wish you had? When you go after something, it will not always work out how you imagine, but you will never truly know unless you try. Go for it, and if you don't succeed, go for it again.

REFLECTION QUESTIONS

1. **Galatians 1–6:** In Galatians 1:10, Paul asks if he is trying to win over human beings or God. What is your answer to this question?

2. **Ephesians 1–6:** What does the Unity in the Body of Christ mean to you?

3. **Philippians 1–4:** In Philippians 3, Paul talks of values and priorities. What priorities are you going after right now?

4. **Colossians 1–4:** Paul talks of suffering for God's people. How do you feel about this?

5. **1 Thessalonians 1–5:** Paul wrote this letter to encourage believers. How have you encouraged others lately?

6. **2 Thessalonians 1–3:** 2 Thessalonians highlights misconceptions the church had about spiritual matters. Do you think Paul's letter helped bring clarity?

____

____

POINTS TO PONDER

1. "Brothers and sisters, I myself don't think I've reached it, but I do this one thing: I forget about the things behind me and reach out for the things ahead of me" (Philippians 3:13). What does this verse mean to you? What's hard about doing as Paul did?
2. Does the letter from Paul to the church of Galatians from this week's readings feel and sound different from other letters? If so, in what ways?
3. Has obeying the expectations of others caused you not to go after something you want? How so?

ACTIVITY

There are many women in history and our own lives who have gone after their dreams! Call to mind an example of a woman who has inspired you to go after something new in your own life. It could be someone from the history books, someone well-known living today, or an inspiring relative or friend you have known personally.

GUIDED PRAYER

Dear God, help me get out of my own way and go after all the things you have for me. Amen.

WEEK 50

USE YOUR GIFT

READINGS

Reading 1: 1 Timothy 1–6

Reading 2: 2 Timothy 1–4

Reading 3: Titus 1–3

Reading 4: Philemon 1

Reading 5: 1 Peter 1–5

Reading 6: 2 Peter 1–3

IT'S HARD TO BE COMFORTABLE IN YOUR GIFTS when there are so many people trying to control and dictate what you do. I can bet you have experienced mistreatment and your gifts have sometimes gone unappreciated and overlooked. There have probably even been times when people ignored your greatness. This can sometimes lead to discouragement and confusion. We are not as motivated to share our gifts with the world.

Paul writes his second letter to his faithful companion and missionary, Timothy, from a damp Roman prison cell before his death. During this time, Christians were scapegoated for the troubles of Rome by the emperor Nero. Paul understands that the ministry will only become more difficult for Timothy, so he offers the pastor instruction and encouragement to continue fulfilling his purpose. In 2 Timothy 1:6–7, he writes, "Because of this, I'm reminding you to revive God's gift that is in you through the laying on of my hands. God didn't give us a spirit that is timid but one that is powerful, loving, and self-controlled."

Remember, your gift is powerful. Your gift is a responsibility. Your gift helps you realize your purpose. Don't let the actions of others force you to hide your gifts from the world. The world desperately needs what only you can create. Use your gift.

REFLECTION QUESTIONS

1. **1 Timothy 1–6:** How does 1 Timothy help us see how gifts come with responsibilities?

2. **2 Timothy 1–4:** In 2 Timothy 1:5, the names of ancestors are mentioned. How can we better understand our gifts today by remembering those of our ancestors?

3. **Titus 1–3:** Titus 3:9 tells us to avoid stupid controversies and fights. Have there been times when controversies or drama turned you away from your gifts?

4. **Philemon 1:** What message do you see in the book of Philemon about hierarchy and equality?

5. **1 Peter 1–5:** What does 1 Peter 1:13 tell us about the importance of faith and hope?

6. **2 Peter 1–3:** How do you feel 2 Peter differs from 1 Peter?

POINTS TO PONDER

1. What was your favorite verse from this week's readings and why?
2. Should you pursue everything you are good at? Why or why not?
3. Who helped you identify your gifts? How has God revealed these gifts to you?

VERSE OF THE WEEK

Our gifts and talents come in many different forms. Consider how you plan to use one of your gifts in light of the message from 1 Peter 4:10: "Serve each other according to the gift each person has received, as good managers of God's diverse gifts."

GUIDED PRAYER

Dear God, thank you for my gifts. Give me wisdom to know how and when to use my gifts for your glory. Amen.

WEEK 51

IF YOU LOVE GOD, PROVE IT

READINGS

Reading 1: Hebrews 1–7

Reading 2: Hebrews 8–13

Reading 3: James 1–5

Reading 4: 1 John 1–5

Reading 5: 2 John 1; 3 John 1

Reading 6: Jude 1

EVERYONE SHOULD KNOW HOW IT FEELS to be loved and to love. Love is special, even if it can feel complicated at times. If we're honest, we sometimes only know how to show love the way we've experienced it. At times, we can block love and even feel undeserving of it. To receive love that may sound and look unfamiliar takes vulnerability and curiosity.

Love should always help us grow. It should make us want to care for others. Love, true love, pushes us closer to God. It leads to action, and action leads to faith. In 1 John 4, John emphasizes to his readers that if we love God, we have to do more than simply say it—we must prove it in our deeds and in our service to others.

Elsewhere in the Bible, 1 Corinthians 13:4–5 teaches us that "love is patient, love is kind, it isn't jealous, it doesn't brag, it isn't arrogant, it isn't rude, it doesn't seek its own advantage, it isn't irritable, it doesn't keep a record of complaints." Love goes far beyond words and objects. Love is present daily in our lives, from how we treat our loved ones to how we care for strangers. Love always points to God.

REFLECTION QUESTIONS

1. **Hebrews 1–7:** What do you learn about angels in these chapters?

2. **Hebrews 8–13:** Hebrews 11:6 tells us that "without faith it is impossible to please God" (NIV). How do you preserve and strengthen your faith?

3. **James 1–5:** In 1 John 4:18, we are reminded, "There is no fear in love, but perfect love drives out fear, because fear expects punishment." Have you experienced fear when trying to love others?

4. **1 John 1–5:** What does 1 John 3 teach you about love?

5. **2 John 1; 3 John 1:** 2 John 1:6 tells us to "live in love." What does this look like in your life?

6. **Jude 1:** What warnings do you see in the book of Jude?

____

____

POINTS TO PONDER

1. The greatest commandment is love. How should love feel?
2. Why do you think love sometimes feels hard?
3. We read in 1 John 4:12, "No one has ever seen God. If we love each other, God remains in us and his love is made perfect in us." What does this verse mean to you?

ACTION OF THE WEEK

Reflect on this week's readings in relation to the theme of love and think of three practical ways you can show more love to others in the week ahead. It might be displaying small acts of love to certain people in your life or through your actions more generally.

GUIDED PRAYER

To the One who is able to protect me from falling, to the One who watches over me, thank you for your love that passes all understanding. Amen.

WEEK 52

ACCESS GRANTED

READINGS

Reading 1: Revelation 1–3

Reading 2: Revelation 4–7

Reading 3: Revelation 8–11

Reading 4: Revelation 12–15

Reading 5: Revelation 16–19

Reading 6: Revelation 20–22

IN ORDER TO ENTER CERTAIN SPACES, we might need a special code or to wait for someone to let us in. We never really know if access will be granted.

In Revelation 3:8, John quotes Jesus in saying, "I know all the things you do, and I have opened a door for you that no one can close" (NLT). Here, Jesus reminds us that God has already granted us access to what we need. We have the permission to enter our new Jerusalem, to stand firm on our beliefs, and to follow God through the open door. Access is granted.

REFLECTION QUESTIONS

1. **Revelation 1–3:** What does Revelation 3:7 mean to you? ("Whatever he opens, no one will shut; and whatever he shuts, no one opens.")

2. **Revelation 4–7:** These chapters offer visions of heaven. Do you believe we can experience such divinity on Earth? If so, how?

____

____

3. **Revelation 12–15:** In what ways do you see God's protection in these chapters?

____

____

POINTS TO PONDER

1. What reoccurring themes did you notice in the book of Revelations?
2. Revelations offers hope to those who are faithful in Christ. How does this message resonate with you?
3. How do we know when God has shut or opened a door for us?

VERSE OF THE WEEK

"'I am the Alpha and the Omega,' says the Lord God, 'the one who is and was and is coming, the Almighty'" (Revelation 1:8). Contemplate how this verse empowers you to move forward in your life.

GUIDED PRAYER

Powerful and loving God, thank you that you have given me the tools and keys to access the places you have for me. It is in your willing love and instructions I believe. Amen.

A FINAL WORD

WOW, YOU MADE IT to the end of this rewarding journey. This is a wonderful accomplishment—congratulations!

The Bible should push us to new places, and it does not have to be our only resource. Read other books in other areas of study to develop what you've learned through this process. Think about the areas that stretched you and made you raise your eyebrows. Take time to study the scriptures and find new and creative meanings for your life. Regardless of our age or what we already know, we all have room to grow. There is always something new to learn, and there are always new places to reach.

You have permission to create more spaces for you and other women to grow—to be better people and create and embrace a better world. I am praying that all those who read these words find the power in themselves and in God to lean into something new for their lives. Always remember that the Bible should free, not oppress us, and God can never be confined to one book or space.

Your new will be glorious—I prayed for it.

In solidarity and love,
Rev. Brittini L. Palmer

RESOURCES

Just a Sister Away: A Womanist Vision of Women's Relationships in the Bible
This book provides a scholarly perspective on various stories of women in the Bible. Written by Dr. Renita Weems, it helps women from various walks of life embrace the Bible in new ways.

Life Application Study Bible: New Living Translation
This study Bible helps readers work through difficult texts and applies everyday examples and illustrations to assist you as you read.

The New Interpreter's Bible
This series of commentary breaks down every book in the Bible, providing historical context, information about the authors, and so much more. Edited by Leander E. Keck, the set offers a fascinating dive into biblical times.

Women's Bible Commentary
This enlightening Bible commentary is written by women scholars Carol Newsom, Sharon H. Ringe, and Jacqueline E. Lapsley for women readers. The various scriptures concerning women that aren't typically addressed during a Sunday morning worship service or Bible study lesson can be found in this commentary.

REFERENCES

Fretheim, Terence E. "Genesis." In *The New Interpreter's Bible*, 7th edition, edited by Leander E. Keck. Nashville, TN: Abingdon Press, 1994.

Newsom, Carol, Sharon H. Ringe, and Jacqueline E. Lapsley, eds. *Women's Bible Commentary: Revised and Updated*. Louisville, KY: Westminster John Knox Press, 2012.

Weems, Renita. *Just a Sister Away: A Womanist Vision of Women's Relationships in the Bible*. Philadelphia, PA: Innisfree Press, Inc., 1988.

NOTES

INDEX

H

I

J

K

L

M

Z

ACKNOWLEDGMENTS

I thank all the women who have prayed, walked, and talked with me throughout this process. I thank Tabernacle Baptist Church, Sixth Mount Zion Baptist Church, Lakewood Church of Hope, and the RISE Together Mentorship Network for giving me opportunities to learn and exercise my gifts. Thank you to my mother, father, family, mentors, professors, and friends for your encouragement. I thank God for God's wisdom and for carrying me through all my dreams and endeavors.

ABOUT THE AUTHOR

Rev. Brittini L. Palmer is a writer, preacher, and communications consultant. She is a graduate of Virginia Union University and McAfee School of Theology. As the founder of Black Women Write for Freedom, she provides writing and consulting services to individuals, organizations, businesses, and universities dedicated to social justice. She supports several organizations, including the RISE Together Mentorship Network, which empowers women of color in ministry, as well as the Interfaith Children's Movement and Sema Films, among others. She has written for various outlets including *Sojourners*, *Penn Live*, and *Baptist News Global*. You can connect with her on social media platforms @BrittiniLPalmer.

www.ingramcontent.com/pod-product-compliance
Lightning Source LLC
LaVergne TN
LVHW070311070626
840604LV00011B/20
9798886083866